Building a Secure Linux Intranet & Internet:

A Complete Guide to Linux Server Networking for the Home or Small Business

Written by, Lynne Kolestar

Table of Contents

Introduction

Why use a Linux server as a home router/firewall?

Using a Linux server as a home router and firewall offers significant advantages over traditional consumer-grade routers, especially when combined with the speed and reliability of a fiber-optic internet connection. One of the key benefits of using Linux is the flexibility and control it provides. Unlike off-the-shelf routers, which often come with limited customization options, a Linux-based router allows you to tailor every aspect of your network configuration to meet your specific needs. Additionally, you can repurpose a regular PC to build your Linux server, making it a cost-effective and powerful solution.

Whether it's advanced traffic filtering, setting up a VPN, or managing traffic prioritization through Quality of Service (QoS), Linux gives you the power to optimize and secure your home network. This customization is particularly appealing to tech enthusiasts or professionals who want granular control over their network's performance and security.

Security is another compelling reason to use a Linux server as a home router/firewall. Linux is renowned for its robust and stable security, particularly when configured properly. By utilizing firewall tools such as iptables or nftables, you can implement advanced security features like stateful packet inspection, preventing unauthorized access, and protecting your network from common cyberattacks such as Distributed Denial of Service (DDoS), port scanning, or brute-force attempts.

With tools like Fail2Ban, you can monitor and automatically respond to unauthorized access attempts, adding another layer of protection to your home network. Additionally, using a Linux server means you're not dependent on a vendor's firmware updates—you can manually patch vulnerabilities and secure your system in real-time.

Moreover, setting up a Linux server as your router/firewall is an excellent learning opportunity, providing hands-on experience with networking principles. This DIY approach can also save money in the long run and encourages sustainability by repurposing older hardware for modern uses. For users managing dynamic IP addresses, Linux also supports Dynamic DNS (DDNS), enabling continuous access to your network even if your public IP changes frequently. Overall, a Linux-based router offers unmatched control, security, and educational benefits for managing your home network.

When combined with a fiber-optic connection, these advantages are even more pronounced. Fiber-optic internet provides ultra-fast data transfer rates, often exceeding 1 Gbps, and a Linux server can handle this speed efficiently. By routing traffic from the fiber Optical Network Terminal (ONT)—which converts the fiber signal to Ethernet—through its WAN interface, a Linux server can deliver high-speed internet to your entire home network. By equipping the server with Gigabit Ethernet or faster Network Interface Cards (NICs), you can fully exploit the bandwidth fiber-optic internet offers, ensuring smooth and high-performance connectivity across all your devices.

With advanced traffic management tools like QoS, the

server can prioritize bandwidth for essential tasks like video streaming or gaming, ensuring a seamless experience even during high network usage. Additionally, the faster upload speeds offered by fiber-optic internet make advanced firewall configurations even more critical, as they can handle large volumes of traffic without compromising on security. Tools like iptables or nftables excel at filtering traffic and protecting your network from external threats, allowing you to fully leverage the fiber connection's potential without sacrificing security.

By combining the power and flexibility of Linux with the speed of fiber, this setup allows you to control your network in ways consumer-grade routers simply can't match. Whether you're managing multiple devices, hosting services, or securing high-speed connections, using a Linux server as a router and firewall provides the ideal solution for modern home networks equipped with fiber-optic internet.

Flexibility, security, and learning potential of DIY networking

This book serves as a guide to building your own home router and firewall for both intranet and internet use—also known as DIY networking. A Linux-based DIY networking setup offers unmatched flexibility, cost efficiency, security, and valuable learning opportunities, making it the ideal choice for tech enthusiasts, professionals, or anyone seeking full control over their home or small business network. Whether you're managing a website with local or remote access, or an interoffice web-based environment, a Linux setup gives you complete control.

By creating your own network infrastructure using open-source tools and hardware, you can design a system tailored to your specific needs, far beyond what off-the-shelf consumer-grade routers offer. With DIY networking, you are in charge of every element, from configuring advanced firewall rules to managing bandwidth and traffic prioritization, giving you the freedom to optimize network performance according to your unique requirements.

Flexibility is a key benefit of DIY networking. With a Linux-based router, you are not limited by the constraints of proprietary firmware or pre-defined configurations. You can customize network settings, create custom firewall rules, implement advanced routing protocols, and easily integrate VPNs, all with the ability to expand your network as your needs grow.

Want to prioritize bandwidth for gaming or video conferencing while throttling less critical activities? Want to segment your network into virtual LANs (VLANs) to separate traffic for security or performance reasons? With DIY networking, these possibilities are entirely within your control. This flexibility is ideal for power users who require specific configurations that go beyond what a traditional router can provide.

Another major advantage is security. Consumer-grade routers often have limited security features, and you're dependent on the manufacturer for firmware updates, which may not always be timely or available. By using a Linux server as a router/firewall, you can implement robust security measures that are tailored to your network environment. Tools like iptables, nftables, and Fail2Ban allow you to set up stateful firewalls, filter suspicious traffic, and automatically respond to potential security threats. Furthermore, because Linux is open-source, you are not dependent on a vendor to patch vulnerabilities—you can actively maintain and secure your network on your own terms, staying ahead of potential threats. This self-managed security can significantly enhance your network's defense against external attacks, making it especially valuable for privacy-conscious users.

Finally, DIY networking offers substantial learning potential. Setting up and managing a Linux-based router or firewall forces you to engage with networking principles at a much deeper level. You'll learn about routing, subnetting, firewall configurations, network interfaces, and much more—skills that are increasingly valuable in today's tech-driven world. Whether you're an aspiring network engineer or simply a curious enthusiast, building your own network from scratch offers a hands-on learning experience that can't be matched by plug-and-play devices. This kind of self-directed learning can boost your technical confidence and open doors to more advanced networking projects, from creating home servers to setting up complex multi-site VPNs.

DIY networking provides an unmatched level of control, security, and learning opportunities. The freedom to customize your network's infrastructure, the ability to apply advanced security measures, and the educational benefits of working with open-source tools make DIY networking a rewarding pursuit for those seeking to enhance both their technical skills and their home network's capabilities.

Basic understanding of Linux, networking concepts, and hardware.

This book aims to provide a foundational understanding of Linux, networking concepts, and hardware, enabling readers to build and manage robust, efficient, and secure systems. Linux, an open-source operating system, is widely used for servers, desktops, and embedded systems due to its stability, flexibility, and security. Based on the Unix model, Linux offers a command-line interface (CLI) that allows precise control over system configuration. Its open-source nature means users can modify the source code to suit their specific needs, making it an attractive option for those who value customization and control.

Networking concepts are equally crucial for anyone looking to set up and manage a system, whether for personal or business use. Key topics include understanding how devices communicate over a network, with concepts like IP addresses, subnets, and DNS (Domain Name System). The book will cover how to configure routers, firewalls, and network protocols such as TCP/IP to ensure a secure and efficient network. Additionally, best practices for network security, including encryption, VPNs, and access control, will be discussed to protect systems from external threats and secure communication between devices.

On the hardware side, a basic understanding of how computers and servers operate will be covered. This includes knowledge of key components such as the CPU, RAM, storage, and network interfaces, as well as how they interact within a system. Whether repurposing an old PC as a server or configuring new hardware, understanding both hardware and software architecture helps in making informed decisions about system performance, upgrades, and troubleshooting. With this foundational knowledge in Linux, networking, and hardware, readers will be equipped to manage their own systems, set up secure networks, and optimize performance to meet their specific needs.

Chapter 1: Understanding Home Networking

Overview of Network Topology

Home network or intranet components (modem, router, switch, firewall)

A home network, often referred to as an intranet, is a system of interconnected devices that allows you to share resources, such as internet access, files, and printers, within your household or small office. To build an efficient and secure home network, it is crucial to understand the key components that make up the infrastructure: the modem, router, switch, and firewall.

The modem is the device that connects your home network to the internet. It acts as a bridge between your local network and your internet service provider (ISP), converting the signals from the ISP into a format that your devices can use. Modems come in various types, such as cable, DSL, or fiber-optic, depending on the type of internet connection your provider offers. The modem typically provides one point of entry for your home network, transmitting data from the internet to your router and vice versa.

The router is the heart of the home network, directing traffic between your devices and the internet. It assigns local IP addresses to each connected device (like computers, smartphones, and printers) and routes data packets to the correct destination, either within the local network or to the wider internet. Modern routers often include built-in wireless capabilities (Wi-Fi), allowing you to connect devices without physical cables. A router also has security features, such as Network Address Translation (NAT) and basic firewall protection, to safeguard the network from external threats.

A switch is used in larger home networks or setups with multiple wired devices. It serves as a central point for connecting devices within your local network, such as computers, printers, and servers. Unlike a router, which connects to the internet, a switch facilitates communication between devices on the same network, improving data flow and efficiency. While routers generally have a few Ethernet ports, a switch expands the number of devices that can be physically connected via Ethernet cables, ensuring reliable, high-speed connections for devices that require a wired setup.

Lastly, a firewall is essential for protecting your home network from external threats. It acts as a barrier between your internal network and the internet, monitoring incoming and outgoing traffic to block any potentially harmful or unauthorized access. Firewalls can be implemented in various ways, including software-based firewalls running on individual devices or hardware-based firewalls integrated into your router. A firewall helps prevent cyberattacks, such as hacking attempts, malware, and viruses, ensuring that only legitimate traffic is allowed into your network.

One of the key advantages of using a Linux-based system for your home network is its inherent resistance to viruses and malware. Unlike more commonly targeted operating systems like Windows, Linux is less susceptible to viruses due to its robust security architecture and lower profile in terms of widespread consumer use. Most malware is written to target Windows-based systems, which makes Linux a safer choice for those looking to secure their home network. Additionally, the open-source nature of Linux allows the community to quickly identify and patch vulnerabilities, contributing to its high level of security.

When combined with a Linux firewall, your home network (intranet) can be completely protected. Linux firewalls, such as iptables or ufw (Uncomplicated Firewall), offer powerful ways to control traffic and prevent unauthorized access to your internal network. These firewalls can be finely tuned to allow only specific types of communication while blocking all other potentially harmful traffic. Since Linux has strong user permissions and security controls, a well-configured Linux firewall can act as a formidable defense against external threats, ensuring that only trusted data is allowed to pass through and keeping the network safe from intrusion. By utilizing both the inherent security of Linux and an effective firewall, you can create a highly secure, low-risk home network environment.

Together, these components form the backbone of a secure and functional home network. Understanding how each part works and how they interact is crucial for setting up, maintaining, and securing your network, whether you're just connecting a few devices or creating a more complex home intranet with advanced features.

DHCP vs. Static IP addressing

When setting up a network, one of the key decisions is how to assign IP addresses to devices within the network. The two primary methods for assigning IP addresses are DHCP (Dynamic Host Configuration Protocol) and Static IP addressing. Each method has its own advantages and use cases, depending on the network's needs and the devices being used.

DHCP is a protocol that automatically assigns IP addresses to devices on a network. When a device connects to the network, the DHCP server allocates an available IP address from a predefined pool and provides it to the device, along with other network configuration information, such as the default gateway and DNS servers. This process is entirely automated, which makes it convenient for home networks, large networks, or any environment where devices frequently join and leave the network. For example, laptops, smartphones, and tablets are typically configured to use DHCP, as they often connect to different networks and require automatic IP address assignment.

One of the main benefits of DHCP is its simplicity and cost-effectiveness. By automating the assignment of IP addresses, it eliminates the need for manual configuration, reducing the risk of errors and conflicts. Additionally, it can be more cost-efficient, especially in larger networks, since it requires less administrative effort and fewer resources. Additionally, DHCP allows network administrators to manage a large number of devices more easily, as they don't need to manually assign and track each device's IP address. The protocol also simplifies network maintenance, as devices can automatically receive updated network configurations (e.g., a new DNS server address) without requiring manual intervention.

On the other hand, static IP addressing involves manually assigning a fixed IP address to a device. This method is particularly useful in situations where a device requires a consistent, unchanging IP address, such as when hosting your own website and configuring your domain name to point to your web server. Servers, network printers, and other devices that provide services or need to be reliably located by other devices on the network typically use static IPs. Static IPs are essential for services like web hosting, email servers, and remote access solutions, as they allow users or other devices to consistently reach the server at the same IP address.

The main advantage of static IP addressing is its predictability. Since the device always has the same IP address, it is easier to configure and maintain network services that require a fixed address. For example, a static IP makes it easier to set up port forwarding for remote access or to establish secure connections, as you don't have to worry about the address changing over time. Static IPs are also necessary for network devices like routers and firewalls, which need a fixed address for proper operation.

However, static IP addressing requires more manual configuration and maintenance. The network administrator must keep track of each assigned address to avoid conflicts, ensuring that no two devices are assigned the same IP. Additionally, in larger networks, managing static IPs can become cumbersome. If too many devices are assigned static IPs, the network can run out of available addresses, particularly if the IP address range is too small.

Ultimately, the choice between DHCP and static IP addressing depends on the specific requirements of the network. For most home networks or devices that don't need to be accessed by a consistent IP address, DHCP is the most convenient and efficient solution. However, for critical devices that provide services or need constant availability, static IP addressing is often the preferred choice. Many networks use a combination of both methods, with DHCP handling devices like laptops and smartphones, and static IPs assigned to servers and other critical network devices.

Public vs. Private IP addresses

In networking, IP addresses are critical for identifying devices and facilitating communication across networks. These addresses can be categorized as either public or private, and each serves a distinct purpose depending on the network environment. Understanding the difference between public and private IP addresses is essential for configuring networks, ensuring security, and managing access to resources.

Public IP addresses are globally unique and can be accessed

over the internet. When you connect to a website or an online service, your device communicates with the service using its public IP address. These addresses are assigned by Internet Service Providers (ISPs) and are required for any device or service that needs to be reachable from outside a local network. For example, web servers, email servers, and other services hosted online must have public IP addresses so that users from anywhere in the world can connect to them. Because they are visible and accessible over the internet, public IP addresses are more vulnerable to external threats, such as hacking attempts, making network security measures, like firewalls, critical in protecting these systems.

Public IP addresses are scarce resources, as there are a limited number of IPv4 addresses available. To address this issue, IPv6 was introduced, providing a much larger pool of IP addresses. However, IPv4 is still widely used, and public IP addresses are typically assigned dynamically by ISPs, meaning they can change periodically unless a static public IP is requested for specific needs, such as hosting a server.

In contrast, private IP addresses are used within local networks, such as home or office networks, and are not routable on the public internet. These addresses allow devices like computers, printers, and smartphones to communicate with each other within the network. Private IP addresses are defined by standards set by the Internet Assigned Numbers Authority (IANA) and fall within specific ranges: 10.0.0.0 to 10.255.255.255, 172.16.0.0 to 172.31.255.255, and 192.168.0.0 to 192.168.255.255. These addresses can be reused across different networks because they are isolated and only function within their local environments. For instance, two devices on separate home networks could both have the private IP address

192.168.1.10 without any conflict since they are part of different private networks.

A key benefit of using private IP addresses is that they help conserve the number of public IP addresses required. Through Network Address Translation (NAT), devices with private IP addresses can communicate with the public internet. NAT, typically implemented on routers, translates the private IP addresses into a public IP address when a device on the local network accesses the internet. This allows multiple devices in a local network to share a single public IP address, reducing the need for a large number of public IPs.

Public IP addresses are necessary for devices that need to be accessible over the internet, while private IP addresses are used within local networks to facilitate internal communication. By leveraging NAT, private IP addresses allow multiple devices to access the internet using a single public IP address, which helps conserve public IPs and adds an extra layer of security to the network. Understanding how public and private IP addresses work together is essential for setting up and managing secure and efficient networks.

Network Address Translation (NAT) and masquerading concepts

Network Address Translation (NAT) is a key networking technology that allows multiple devices on a private network to share a single public IP address when accessing external networks, such as the internet. NAT is primarily used in home and small office networks where multiple devices—such as computers, smartphones, and printers—need to access the internet but only one public IP address is available. This functionality is often implemented on a router, which acts as the gateway between the internal network (using private IP addresses) and the external network (internet).

NAT works by translating the private IP addresses of devices on the internal network to a public IP address when they communicate with external networks. When a device sends a request (e.g., to access a website), the router replaces the device's private IP address with its own public IP address. It then forwards the request to the destination (the website server). The router also keeps track of which device initiated the request so that when the response comes back, it can translate the public IP address back to the correct private IP and send the data to the appropriate device. This process happens seamlessly, allowing devices within the private network to interact with external networks without requiring a unique public IP for each device.

There are different types of NAT, including Static NAT, Dynamic NAT, and Port Address Translation (PAT), also known as NAT Overload. Static NAT maps a single public IP address to a specific private IP address, which is useful for servers that need to be consistently reachable from outside the network. Dynamic NAT, on the other hand, uses a pool of public IP addresses and dynamically assigns one to each device as needed. PAT, or NAT Overload, is the most commonly used version of NAT in home networks. It allows multiple devices to share a single public IP address by using different ports to track individual sessions. This means that multiple internal devices can communicate over the same public IP address, but the router keeps the sessions separate using port numbers.

Masquerading is a specialized form of NAT often associated with Linux-based systems, where it serves a similar purpose to PAT. Like NAT Overload, masquerading allows many devices on a private network to access the internet using a single public IP address. When masquerading is enabled on a Linux router or firewall, it dynamically maps outgoing traffic from private IP addresses to the public IP address assigned to the router, while also keeping track of each device's session. The main difference between masquerading and regular NAT is that masquerading is typically used for dynamic public IP addresses, such as those assigned by ISPs that change periodically.

Masquerading is especially popular in Linux environments where users configure routers or firewalls using tools like iptables, the built-in firewall utility in many Linux distributions. With masquerading, a simple configuration can enable multiple devices to use a single internet connection, making it an essential tool for small office or home networks that rely on Linux-based systems.

NAT and masquerading provide several key benefits. First, they help conserve public IP addresses, which are a limited resource, by allowing multiple devices to share a single public IP. This is particularly important for home networks, small businesses, or any environment where purchasing multiple public IP addresses would be impractical. Second, they add an additional layer of security by hiding internal IP addresses from external networks. Devices on the private network are not directly exposed to the public internet, reducing the chances of external attacks. Only the router's public IP address is visible, making it harder for hackers to directly target individual devices on the private network.

NAT and masquerading are fundamental technologies that enable efficient, secure internet access for multiple devices within a private network. By translating private IP addresses into a public one and vice versa, these techniques ensure seamless communication between local networks and external systems, while helping to manage IP resources and enhance security. Whether used in a home network, small business, or larger enterprise, understanding and implementing NAT and masquerading are critical for efficient network management.

How Routers and Firewalls Work

Role of routers in directing traffic

Routers and firewalls are critical components in any network, each serving distinct but complementary roles in managing traffic and ensuring security. A router's primary function is to direct traffic between different networks, while a firewall protects a network by controlling which types of traffic are allowed in or out. Together, these devices help create a secure and efficient environment for communication, whether in a home, business, or larger network setup.

A router acts as a traffic director, forwarding data packets between different networks based on their destination IP addresses. For example, when a device in your home network attempts to access a website, the router determines the best path for the data to travel between your local network and the internet. Routers use routing tables to make these decisions, selecting the most efficient route to deliver data from point A to point B. In a home network, the router sits between your private network and your Internet Service Provider (ISP), managing all the traffic that goes in and out. Routers also assign IP addresses to devices on the local network using DHCP (Dynamic Host Configuration Protocol) and ensure that these devices can communicate with each other seamlessly.

Routers play a vital role in managing both local traffic within the network (intranet) and traffic that travels between the internal network and external systems, such as the internet. They ensure that devices like computers, smartphones, and smart appliances can all communicate effectively while maintaining a connection to the outside world. In more complex setups, routers can also manage Virtual Local Area Networks (VLANs), separating network traffic for different types of devices or users. This separation can help reduce congestion and improve security by segmenting sensitive traffic from general internet usage.

While routers manage traffic, firewalls are responsible for securing the network by controlling the flow of incoming and outgoing data. A firewall acts as a barrier between the trusted internal network and potentially harmful external networks, like the internet. It inspects all data packets that attempt to enter or leave the network, deciding whether to allow, block, or filter them based on predefined security rules. Firewalls are essential in preventing unauthorized access, malware, or other security threats from infiltrating the network.

For a home network, firewalls can be implemented either as software (on individual devices) or as hardware (built into routers). Many modern routers include basic firewall functionality to protect the entire network, though more advanced configurations might require dedicated firewall devices. Packet filtering, one of the key methods used by firewalls, analyzes packets based on their source and destination IP addresses, port numbers, and the protocol being used. This allows the firewall to block suspicious or unwanted traffic, such as attempts to access the network from untrusted sources.

Firewalls also help protect against common cyber threats like Distributed Denial of Service (DDoS) attacks, where an external attacker tries to overwhelm the network by flooding it with traffic. By monitoring traffic patterns and identifying anomalies, firewalls can automatically block suspicious activity before it becomes a serious issue. For home networks, a firewall is essential in keeping sensitive data, like personal information, financial transactions, and smart device communications, safe from external threats.

Routers and firewalls work together to ensure the smooth and secure operation of a home network. Routers handle the efficient transmission of data between different devices and networks, while firewalls monitor and control access, preventing unauthorized or malicious traffic from entering the network. Together, they provide both connectivity and protection, forming the backbone of a secure and well-functioning home network.

Importance of firewalls in protecting home networks

Firewalls are a critical component in securing home networks, serving as the first line of defense against external threats. As more devices in the modern household connect to the internet—ranging from computers and smartphones to smart appliances and security systems—protecting the network from malicious actors becomes increasingly important. A firewall acts as a barrier between your internal network (the devices in your home) and the wider internet, controlling incoming and outgoing traffic based on security rules. This helps prevent unauthorized access, malware, and other cyber threats from compromising your data and devices.

One of the primary functions of a firewall is to monitor and filter traffic. Firewalls analyze all data packets that attempt to enter or leave your network and decide whether to allow, block, or restrict them based on predefined security rules. This filtering process is crucial for protecting your home network from threats like hacking attempts, phishing, and malware. Without a firewall, your network is exposed to direct communication from the internet, making it easier for malicious actors to exploit vulnerabilities in your devices. A properly configured firewall ensures that only trusted traffic is allowed through, while suspicious or unrecognized traffic is blocked or closely monitored.

For home users, a firewall also provides protection from remote access threats. Many attackers attempt to remotely access home networks by scanning for open ports or exploiting weak passwords and outdated software. A firewall helps block these attempts by limiting access to specific services and closing off non-essential ports that hackers often target. This level of control helps prevent unauthorized access to sensitive devices, such as home security cameras, smart locks, or personal computers, which are common targets for cybercriminals.

Another key role of firewalls is preventing malware from entering your home network. Whether through malicious downloads, infected email attachments, or compromised websites, malware is a significant threat to home users. Once malware infiltrates your network, it can steal personal information, corrupt files, or even take control of your devices in the case of ransomware. A firewall can help mitigate these risks by identifying and blocking known malicious traffic or suspicious behavior, reducing the chances of malware spreading across your devices. By combining firewalls with antivirus software and regular security updates, you create a more comprehensive defense system against these types of attacks.

Network segmentation is another advantage of firewalls in a home environment. In larger home networks, firewalls can help create separate zones or sub-networks, isolating different devices for added security. For example, smart home devices such as thermostats, cameras, or speakers can be placed in a separate network from your computers or personal devices. This segmentation means that even if an attacker compromises one part of the network, they won't have unrestricted access to all your devices and data. Firewalls make it possible to manage and enforce these zones, providing an additional layer of security for your most sensitive information.

Firewalls are essential for protecting home networks from a wide range of cyber threats. By monitoring and controlling traffic, blocking unauthorized access, preventing malware, and enabling network segmentation, firewalls provide a critical layer of security that keeps your devices and data safe. In today's increasingly connected homes, where every device is a potential point of vulnerability, a well-configured firewall is a fundamental tool for safeguarding privacy and maintaining the integrity of your home network.

Firewall principles: filtering traffic, stateful packet inspection

Firewalls are vital in network security, operating based on a set of core principles that govern how they filter and control traffic. At their most basic level, firewalls act as gatekeepers between your internal network and external networks, such as the internet. One of the fundamental tasks of a firewall is traffic filtering, which involves inspecting data packets as they enter and exit the network and deciding whether to allow or block them based on predefined rules. These rules can be based on several factors, such as the source and destination IP addresses, port numbers, and the type of protocol used (e.g., TCP, UDP). This process helps ensure that only legitimate, authorized data is allowed to communicate with your network, while suspicious or potentially harmful traffic is blocked before it can cause damage.

Traffic filtering is often categorized into two main types: packet filtering and stateful packet inspection (SPI). In packet filtering, the firewall examines each data packet individually without considering the context of the communication session. It analyzes the packet header information, such as the source/destination addresses and port numbers, and compares it against a set of rules. If the packet matches an allowed rule, it is permitted through; otherwise, it is blocked. While this method is simple and efficient, it has limitations in its ability to fully detect more sophisticated or multi-step attacks, as it doesn't track the overall state of a connection.

To address this limitation, modern firewalls often employ a more advanced technique called stateful packet inspection (SPI). SPI not only checks individual packets but also keeps track of the state of active connections, allowing the firewall to make decisions based on the context of the entire communication session. For example, when a device inside the network initiates a request to a server on the internet, SPI ensures that the response from the server is part of the expected session before allowing it through. This method offers a deeper layer of security by ensuring that all incoming traffic is related to legitimate outgoing requests, and it can more effectively block unsolicited or malicious traffic that might attempt to mimic legitimate connections.

By maintaining a state table that tracks each active session, stateful firewalls are able to prevent a range of attacks that would otherwise bypass simpler packet-filtering mechanisms. This approach is especially effective against certain types of threats, such as spoofing (where attackers disguise their traffic to appear as though it is coming from a trusted source) and Denial-of-Service (DoS) attacks, which flood the network with illegitimate traffic in an attempt to overwhelm it. Since SPI monitors the state of each connection, it can detect and block traffic that doesn't conform to established patterns of legitimate communication.

Firewalls use traffic filtering and stateful packet inspection as key principles to protect networks from unauthorized access and malicious activity. While packet filtering provides a basic level of protection by examining individual packets, stateful packet inspection adds a more sophisticated layer of security by tracking ongoing communication sessions and ensuring that only valid, expected traffic is allowed into the network. Together, these mechanisms form the backbone of firewall security, ensuring that home and business networks remain protected against evolving cyber threats.

Chapter 2: Hardware Requirements and Network Layout

Selecting Hardware for Your Server

Minimum hardware requirements (CPU, RAM, network interface cards)

While nearly any desktop computer can be repurposed to run a Linux server, it's important to ensure the machine's internal components meet the demands of your intended use. With a bit of research, outdated components in older desktops can often be easily upgraded or replaced to improve performance. Many suppliers offer both new and used internal parts, available online and in stores. Selecting the right hardware is crucial for achieving optimal performance, reliability, and scalability, ensuring your server can handle workloads efficiently and operate smoothly over time.

While the exact hardware requirements will vary based on the intended use of the server, it is important to consider several key components: the CPU (Central Processing Unit), RAM (Random Access Memory), and network interface cards (NICs). These components are fundamental to the server's ability to handle processing tasks, multitasking, and managing network traffic effectively.

CPU (Central Processing Unit)

The CPU is the brain of your server, responsible for executing instructions and running applications. When selecting a CPU, it's essential to match its capabilities to the workload your server will handle. For a basic home server or small business setup, such as hosting a website or managing file storage, a dual-core processor or even a low-power CPU like Intel's Atom or AMD's Ryzen 3 could be sufficient. However, for more demanding tasks such as virtualization, database management, or media streaming, you'll want a more powerful CPU with multiple cores and higher clock speeds, such as an Intel Core i5/i7 or AMD Ryzen 5/7 series.

If you plan on running many simultaneous services or virtual machines, you might even consider server-grade processors like Intel Xeon or AMD EPYC, which are designed for handling heavy multitasking and large data workloads.

RAM (Random Access Memory)

RAM plays a crucial role in the server's performance, particularly when running multiple services or applications concurrently. RAM temporarily stores data that the CPU can access quickly, reducing the time spent retrieving information from slower storage devices. For a basic server setup, at least 4GB of RAM is recommended, but this can increase depending on the server's role. For instance, if you are running a database server, web hosting multiple sites, or operating in a virtualized environment, 8GB to 16GB of RAM may be required to ensure smooth performance without bottlenecks. Higher memory capacities are especially important when dealing with high traffic loads or running several resource-intensive services. Ensuring that your server has adequate RAM will improve response times and allow your system to handle multiple users or requests without slowing down.

Network Interface Cards (NICs)

Network Interface Cards (NICs) connect your server to a network, and their performance is crucial for managing network traffic. Most modern motherboards come with built-in NICs that support gigabit Ethernet (1 Gbps), which is sufficient for most home or small business servers. However, if your server needs to handle high volumes of traffic or you are setting up a server that will serve a large number of users or devices (e.g., as a media server or for cloud storage), you might want to invest in multiple NICs or upgrade to a faster card, such as 10 Gbps Ethernet. Having multiple NICs can also enable features like network redundancy and load balancing, which improve reliability by allowing traffic to be distributed across multiple connections or providing backup in case one connection fails.

Additionally, consider the quality of the NIC drivers when selecting a card, as poorly supported or outdated drivers can lead to network instability. Ensure that your NICs are compatible with your chosen operating system (such as Linux or Windows Server) to avoid potential issues down the line.

Additional Considerations

When selecting hardware, it's also important to think about storage. While not directly tied to the performance of the CPU, RAM, or NICs, storage is crucial for data retention and access. Many servers benefit from using solid-state drives (SSDs) for faster read/write speeds compared to traditional hard drives (HDDs), particularly for frequently accessed data. If budget allows, consider a combination of SSDs for the operating system and critical services, and larger HDDs for long-term storage.

Selecting the appropriate hardware for your server is crucial for ensuring it can handle your specific needs efficiently. By choosing the right CPU for processing power, ensuring enough RAM for multitasking, and having robust NICs for network connectivity, you can create a reliable and capable server that can manage your home or small business's networking and computing demands.

Network Interface Cards (NICs) for WAN (external) and LAN (internal) connections

When setting up a server or router for networking, the Network Interface Card (NIC) plays a crucial role in connecting the server to both the external internet (WAN) and internal local network (LAN). The NIC enables communication between the server and the network by sending and receiving data packets. In more advanced configurations—such as those used for setting up a firewall or router—it's common to have multiple NICs, one for the WAN (internet connection) and another for the LAN (internal network connection). In this setup, each NIC is tasked with handling specific types of traffic. The WAN NIC connects the server to the internet, while the LAN NIC facilitates communication between devices within the local network.

Example: Setting up a Linux Server with Multiple NICs

Consider a typical Linux-based router or firewall setup using two NICs:

eth0 (WAN): This NIC connects to the internet through a modem or ISP (Internet Service Provider). It handles all external traffic between the local network and the outside world, and it's typically assigned a public IP address from your ISP.

eth1 (LAN): This NIC connects to the internal network, typically through a switch, to manage all communication between devices (like desktops, laptops, and other networked devices) inside your home or office. This NIC generally uses private IP addresses (such as those in the 192.168.x.x range) to create the internal network.

With this configuration, the Linux server acts as both a router and firewall. The server forwards traffic between the WAN (eth0) and LAN (eth1), while simultaneously monitoring and filtering traffic to ensure security.

How Internal Devices Access the Internet

In this setup, devices on your intranet (LAN), such as desktops or smartphones, will need to access the internet through the Linux firewall.

Here's how it works:

Internal Device Requests: A device on the LAN (e.g., a desktop computer with an IP address like 192.168.1.10) will initiate an internet request, such as browsing a website. The request is first sent to the internal LAN NIC (eth1).

Firewall Routing and Address Translation: The Linux server, acting as the firewall and router, receives the traffic on eth1 and routes it to eth0, the external NIC. However, since the device has a private IP address (e.g., 192.168.1.10), the server must translate this private address to the public IP address assigned to eth0 before sending the request out to the internet. This process is called Network Address Translation (NAT).

NAT and Masquerading: The server uses masquerading (a form of NAT) to ensure that the outgoing request appears to come from the server's public IP address rather than the private IP address of the internal device. This is done by modifying the source address of the outgoing packets. The server tracks the connection, and when the response from the internet arrives, it knows which internal device to send it to, based on the port number used in the original request.

Internet Response: The response from the internet (e.g., the website data) comes to the Linux server on eth0 (the public NIC). The server uses its routing table to determine that the response should be sent to the appropriate device on the internal network (via eth1). The server unpacks the response, performs any necessary filtering through the firewall rules, and forwards the data to the correct internal device, completing the round trip.

Example Flow:

A device on your LAN (e.g., 192.168.1.10) requests access to a website.

The Linux firewall/router forwards the request through eth1 (internal network) to eth0 (external network).

The public IP of eth0 is used to request the website from the internet.

The website responds to the public IP of eth0, and the server forwards the data back to the requesting device (192.168.1.10) on the internal network, over eth1.

Role of Firewall in Securing the Connection

The firewall plays an essential role in controlling the traffic flowing between the internal network (eth1) and the internet (eth0). Here's how it protects your LAN:

Traffic Filtering: The Linux firewall inspects both incoming and outgoing traffic, enforcing rules that determine what kind of traffic is allowed to pass between the internal and external networks. For example, the firewall might block all incoming traffic except for HTTP (port 80) and HTTPS (port 443), allowing only web traffic to reach your LAN.

Stateful Packet Inspection: The firewall also uses stateful packet inspection to monitor the state of active connections. It ensures that only responses to legitimate requests are allowed back into the network, effectively preventing unsolicited or malicious connections from reaching internal devices.

Protection from External Threats: By using a Linux firewall, you can block harmful traffic, such as hacking attempts, DDoS (Distributed Denial of Service) attacks, and malware, ensuring that only legitimate traffic is allowed into your network.

Using multiple NICs—one for the WAN and another for the LAN—on a Linux server or router offers a flexible and secure way to manage network traffic. Devices on the internal network (LAN) can access the internet through the eth1 interface, with the Linux server acting as a gateway. By using NAT and masquerading, the Linux firewall ensures that internal devices can access external resources securely, while simultaneously filtering and controlling traffic to protect the internal network from potential threats. This approach provides not only security but also full control over both your internal and external networking environment.

Repurposing old hardware vs. purchasing new equipment

When setting up a server or network infrastructure, one of the first decisions you'll face is whether to repurpose old hardware or purchase new equipment. Both options have distinct advantages and drawbacks, and the best choice depends on your specific needs, budget, and technical expertise.

Repurposing Old Hardware

Repurposing older hardware—such as desktop computers, laptops, or network devices—can be an excellent way to save money while still setting up a functional server or network. Many older devices still have sufficient processing power, RAM, and storage capacity to serve as an efficient server for smaller-scale applications. This option is particularly attractive for those working within a tight budget or for tech enthusiasts looking for a project.

Repurposing also offers a more sustainable option. Instead of throwing away or discarding old hardware, you can give it a second life, reducing e-waste and making use of perfectly functional components. For instance, an old desktop computer with a decent CPU and enough RAM can be easily converted into a home server, firewall, or router with a bit of research and minimal upgrades. Components like storage drives, RAM, and network cards can often be upgraded or replaced for a relatively low cost, which can breathe new life into the machine without the need for a full overhaul.

One of the main advantages of repurposing is the potential for customization. Since you are working with existing hardware, you have the freedom to make incremental improvements, such as adding more storage, upgrading the network interface card (NIC), or replacing faulty components. Repurposing is also a great opportunity to learn more about hardware and gain hands-on experience in hardware repair and optimization.

However, repurposing has its limitations. Older hardware may not support the latest technologies, such as higher-speed network interfaces or modern processors, which can impact performance, especially if you're running more demanding applications. Additionally, the older the hardware, the more likely it is to experience reliability issues, leading to potential downtime or failure if critical components wear out.

Purchasing New Equipment

On the other hand, purchasing new equipment offers several benefits, particularly if you require a system with the latest technology, greater reliability, and higher performance. New hardware often comes with improved energy efficiency, faster processors, and greater memory capacity, ensuring that your server or network can handle more complex tasks, scale easily, and provide long-term support without the risk of failure due to aging components.

New equipment also comes with manufacturer warranties and customer support, which can be a significant advantage for those who want peace of mind knowing that they can easily resolve any issues that arise. With newer hardware, you also have access to the latest innovations in networking, security, and processing technologies, which can be crucial if you're building a system for business use or handling sensitive data.

Purchasing new equipment ensures that you're not limited by the constraints of outdated components. For example, modern NICs support faster network speeds, and newer processors handle more concurrent tasks, allowing for more efficient and robust server performance. If you're planning on running resource-intensive applications like web hosting, video streaming, or virtualization, new hardware will offer the scalability and speed required to meet these demands without the bottlenecks associated with older machines.

However, purchasing new equipment can be significantly more expensive, especially if you're setting up a high-performance server or network infrastructure. In addition to the upfront cost, new devices may require specialized knowledge or additional setup time to optimize for your specific use case. If you don't need cutting-edge performance and your needs are simple, the extra expense of new hardware may not be justified.

Finding the Right Balance

Ultimately, whether to repurpose old hardware or purchase new equipment depends on your needs and budget. If you're setting up a small, personal network or running lightweight applications, repurposing old hardware can be an economical and eco-friendly solution. However, for more demanding setups, where reliability, performance, and scalability are critical, purchasing new equipment may be the better choice.

In many cases, a hybrid approach works well. You can repurpose older hardware for non-critical tasks or for learning purposes while investing in new hardware for core functions such as high-traffic web servers, storage servers, or network firewalls. This way, you can make use of what you already have while ensuring that your critical systems are running on the most reliable and capable hardware.

Physical Network Setup

Connecting modem, server (router), and LAN devices

Setting up a home network or server infrastructure involves connecting several key components: the modem, server (acting as a router), and LAN (Local Area Network) devices. Each plays a distinct role in ensuring efficient and secure communication within your network and with the outside world, such as the internet. Let's break down how to connect and configure these elements, with a focus on how fiber-optic connections are integrated into this setup.

Connecting the Modem

The modem is the device that connects your home or small business network to the internet. It acts as a bridge between the external network provided by your ISP (Internet Service Provider) and your local network. In the case of a fiber-optic connection, the modem is typically a fiber gateway or ONT (Optical Network Terminal), which translates the fiber signal into an Ethernet signal that can be used by your router or server.

To connect the modem:

Fiber Connection: The fiber-optic cable from your ISP should be plugged into the fiber gateway or ONT. Fiber-optic connections provide high-speed internet access with much higher bandwidth and lower latency compared to traditional copper-based connections like DSL or cable. The fiber gateway will have an Ethernet port that connects to the next device in the network.

Power: Ensure that the modem is powered and functioning correctly, with the lights indicating an active connection with your ISP. Fiber connections typically provide faster speeds (up to gigabit speeds in many cases), and the modem should be compatible with this high-speed service.

Connecting the Server (Router)

Next, the server, which can also function as a router, is connected to the modem. The server serves as the central device for routing traffic between the internet and internal network devices (LAN), as well as performing additional tasks such as firewall protection, network address translation (NAT), and even hosting internal services like file sharing or web hosting.

Ethernet Cable to Modem: Use an Ethernet cable to connect the modem's Ethernet port to the network interface card (NIC) on the server. This NIC will likely be labeled as eth0 or enp0s3, depending on your system's configuration.

Configuring as a Router: Once connected, configure the server to act as a router using software like iptables (on Linux) or other routing software. This involves setting up NAT (Network Address Translation) to enable devices on the internal network to communicate with the outside world through the single public IP address provided by the ISP.

Routing and DHCP: The server should also provide DHCP (Dynamic Host Configuration Protocol) services for devices on the local network. DHCP will assign IP addresses automatically to connected devices, ensuring proper network management without manual IP configuration.

Connecting LAN Devices

Once the modem and server are connected, the next step is to link the internal network (LAN) devices. These devices can include computers, laptops, printers, smart TVs, and other network-enabled devices within the home or office.

Wired Connections (Ethernet): If you're using a wired connection for LAN devices, connect each device to the server using an Ethernet cable through a switch (if you need additional ports). The server will route data between the LAN devices and the internet, ensuring they can communicate with each other and access external websites and services.

Wireless Connections (Wi-Fi): If you wish to provide Wi-Fi access for mobile devices or laptops, you can configure the server as a wireless access point (AP) by adding a compatible wireless network interface card (NIC). Alternatively, you can use a dedicated Wi-Fi router connected to the server to provide wireless connectivity.

Fiber to LAN Connectivity: The high-speed fiber connection ensures that any device connected to your LAN network via the server will benefit from faster internet speeds, making this setup ideal for households or small offices with high-bandwidth requirements, such as streaming, gaming, or large file transfers.

Configuring the Network for Security

Security is an important aspect when setting up a home or

office network. The server not only routes traffic but also acts as a firewall to protect your LAN from potential external threats. You can configure iptables or other firewall software on the server to filter incoming and outgoing traffic based on rules you set.

Firewall Configuration: By setting up filtering rules, you can block or allow specific types of traffic, limit external access to only certain ports, and prevent malicious traffic from entering your network. The server should be configured to allow LAN devices to access the internet while blocking unsolicited incoming connections from external sources.

Network Segmentation: If your network is large or you want to keep certain devices separate (such as an IoT network), you can segment your network into different subnets, allowing you to control traffic between different groups of devices.

Testing and Monitoring

Once all devices are connected and configured, it's important to test the network to ensure everything is functioning properly. You can test connectivity to the internet from LAN devices, verify that the server is correctly routing traffic, and check the speed of the internet connection (especially for fiber-optic setups, where you expect high speeds).

Monitoring the network using tools like iftop, netstat, or more advanced network management software can help track traffic, spot any issues, and ensure the network is running optimally.

By connecting the modem, server (router), and LAN devices, you are creating the backbone of your network. In a fiber-optic setup, the high-speed connection allows for smooth data flow, while the server handles routing, security, and network management tasks. Proper configuration ensures that all devices in your network can access the internet securely and efficiently, making it a robust solution for home or small business networks. With the right equipment and configuration, your home network will be both fast and secure, providing excellent connectivity for all your devices.

Basic Network Hardware Setup Example

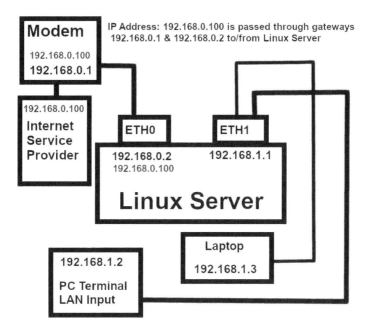

Modem to Linux Server (ETH0):

The ETH0 NIC on your Linux server is connected to the modem via a LAN cable. This will allow the server to communicate with the outside world (internet). In this setup, the server acts as a gateway to route traffic from the internal network (Windows PC) to the internet.

Internal Network Setup (ETH1):

The ETH1 NIC on the Linux server is connected to the external Windows PC via a second LAN cable.

ETH1 serves as the internal network interface, and this NIC will be used to provide network connectivity (both intranet and internet) to the connected Windows PC.

Basic Linux Network Configuration For Windows PC behind Linux Firewall

In many cases, the /etc/network/interfaces file on your Linux server may need to be set up (or modified) to properly configure the network interfaces, particularly if you are using a static IP address or configuring the server to act as a gateway between multiple networks (e.g., for routing and NAT as in your example).

Here's an example setup for the ETH0 and ETH1 interfaces - using a text editor like nano, edit the /etc/network/interfaces file with:

nano /etc/network/interfaces

```
# Loopback network interface
auto lo
iface lo
inet loopback

# For a Dynamic IP or DHCP (changing IP) Setup where ETH0:
# Internet-facing interface connected to the modem
auto eth0
iface eth0
inet dhcp

# Or, for a static IP (unchanging IP) setup where ETH0:
# Internet-facing interface connected to the modem:
# (uncomment or delete '#' at beginning of each line for a
# static IP setup)

# iface eth0 inet static
# address 192.168.0.100    # Your static IP address
# netmask 255.255.255.0    # Standard subnet mask
# gateway 192.168.0.1      # Standard gateway for Linux
# network router

# ETH1: Internal interface connected to the Windows PC
auto eth1
iface eth1 inet static
address 192.168.1.1
netmask 255.255.255.0
```

Basic Linux Server as a Gateway (Routing and NAT):

The Linux server will act as a gateway between the internal network (Windows PC) and the internet by enabling IP forwarding. This allows the server to forward network traffic between the LAN (local network) and the WAN (internet).

To enable IP forwarding on the Linux server, you need to modify the system's configuration files. There are two methods to enable IP forwarding:

Permanent Enabling of IP Forwarding: Modify the /etc/sysctl.conf file to enable IP forwarding permanently. Open the file with a text editor like nano:

nano /etc/sysctl.conf

Add or uncomment the following line:

net.ipv4.ip_forward = 1

After saving the file, apply the changes by running the following command:

sudo sysctl -p

Immediate Enabling of IP Forwarding: If you want to enable IP forwarding immediately (without restarting the server), you can run the following command:

sudo sysctl -w net.ipv4.ip_forward=1

This allows the Linux server to route traffic between the internal network (connected via ETH1) and the external network (connected via ETH0), facilitating internet access for devices on the LAN, such as the Windows PC.

Network Address Translation (NAT):

Since the internal network (ETH1) has a private IP address

(e.g., 192.168.1.2 to 192.168.1.255), the Linux server needs to perform Network Address Translation (NAT) to allow the Windows PC to access the internet using the public IP address provided by the modem.

The server uses iptables to set up NAT on ETH0 (the internet-facing NIC). The basic command for NAT setup is:

sudo iptables -t nat -A POSTROUTING -o eth0 -j MASQUERADE

This command tells the server to masquerade (replace the source address) for outgoing traffic on ETH0.

If iptables is not already installed on your server, you can install the iptables package by running the following commands:

On Debian/Ubuntu-based systems:

sudo apt update

sudo apt install iptables

sudo apt install netfilter-persistent

On Red Hat/CentOS systems:

sudo yum install iptables

sudo yum install netfilter-persistent

After installing and configuring iptables, you'll want to enter the following command:

sudo iptables -t nat -A POSTROUTING -o eth0 -j MASQUERADE

then save the current rules so that they are re-applied after a reboot.

On Debian/Ubuntu-based systems, use the following command to save the rules:

sudo iptables-save > /etc/iptables/rules.v4

On Red Hat/CentOS systems, use the following command:

sudo service iptables save

To make sure that iptables starts automatically at boot, you need to enable the iptables service to start at boot time.

On Debian/Ubuntu-based systems, if you're using the iptables-persistent package, enable it to start on boot:

sudo systemctl enable netfilter-persistent

On Red Hat/CentOS systems, you can enable the iptables service to start on boot with:

sudo systemctl start iptables

Windows PC Network Configuration:

On the Windows PC, you'll configure the network settings as follows:

Set the IP address of the Windows PC to be within the same private subnet as ETH1 (e.g., 192.168.1.2 to 192.168.1.255).

Set the subnet mask to 255.255.255.0 (standard for most private networks).

Set the default gateway to the IP address of the Linux server's ETH1 interface (e.g., 192.168.1.1).

Set the DNS server to a public DNS service (e.g., Google's DNS 8.8.8.8 or your local network's DNS server).

Intranet and Internet Access:

The Windows PC will have intranet access because it's directly connected to the Linux server through ETH1.

The internet access is achieved because the Linux server, acting as a gateway, routes traffic from the Windows PC to the internet through ETH0.

How This Works

Internal Communication: The Windows PC communicates with the Linux server over ETH1 (internal LAN). Since they are on the same subnet, they can easily communicate with each other, forming the intranet.

Internet Access: When the Windows PC requests something from the internet (e.g., browsing a website), it sends the request to the Linux server's ETH1 interface. The Linux server, with its IP forwarding and NAT settings, forwards the request to the modem (via ETH0) and then sends the response back to the Windows PC.

Summary of Configuration:

Linux server:

ETH0: Connected to the modem (internet-facing interface).

ETH1: Connected to the Windows PC (internal network).

Act as a gateway, using IP forwarding and NAT for internet access.

Windows PC:

Set to a static IP address in the same subnet as ETH1.

Default gateway points to the Linux server's ETH1.

DNS points to a public DNS server.

This setup allows the Linux server to route internet traffic for the Windows PC, effectively making the server a bridge between the internal network and the internet. In this configuration, the Windows PC is protected by the Linux firewall. You can further enhance security by adding custom rules to iptables, allowing for more granular control over network traffic.

Chapter 3: Configuring Networking

In a typical Linux system, network interfaces represent the connections through which the computer communicates with the local network or the internet. These interfaces can be physical (like an Ethernet card) or virtual (like a wireless interface or a VPN connection). Each interface has a unique identifier, such as eth0, eth1, wlan0, or lo, which corresponds to a specific network device.

It is crucial to set up iptables or another firewall solution to ensure that network traffic is properly filtered and controlled. Without a firewall in place, even if your network interfaces are correctly configured, your system may not function as expected or could become vulnerable to unauthorized access and attacks from external networks. Please refer to Chapter 4 for further details on firewall configuration.

Identifying Network Interfaces in Linux

To see a list of all network interfaces on your Linux machine, you can use various commands, but the most common ones are ip and ifconfig (though ifconfig is deprecated on many distributions in favor of ip). These commands will provide the necessary information about the interfaces, their IP addresses, and their current status.

Using the ip command:

ip addr show

This command will display detailed information about all available network interfaces. You'll see output that looks like this:

2: eth0: <BROADCAST,MULTICAST,UP,LOWER_UP> mtu 1500 qdisc fq_codel state UP group default qlen 1000

inet 192.168.1.100/24 brd 192.168.1.255 scope global eth0

valid_lft forever preferred_lft forever

In this example, eth0 is the primary network interface, and it has been assigned an IP address of 192.168.1.100. The state UP indicates that the interface is active and operational, while inet shows the IPv4 address assigned to the interface. Keep in mind that your IP address will likely be different and will depend on your Internet Service Provider (ISP), especially if you're using dynamic IP addressing.

Using the ifconfig command:

Ifconfig

The output will look similar to:

eth0: flags=4163<UP,BROADCAST,RUNNING,MULTICAST>
mtu 1500

inet 192.168.1.100 netmask 255.255.255.0 broadcast 192.168.1.255

inet6 fe80::250:56ff:fe89:3e98 prefixlen 64 scopeid 0x20<link>

```
ether 00:50:56:89:3e:98 txqueuelen 1000 (Ethernet)
RX packets 1000 bytes 500000 (500.0 KB)
RX errors 0 dropped 0 overruns 0 frame 0
TX packets 1000 bytes 500000 (500.0 KB)
TX errors 0 dropped 0 overruns 0 carrier 0 collisions 0
```

In this case, eth0 also has the IP address 192.168.1.100, and is ready for communication.

Common Network Interface Names

Linux typically uses the following naming conventions for network interfaces:

Ethernet Interfaces: These are typically named eth0, eth1, etc. (with eth0 being the first Ethernet interface). The number increases if there are additional interfaces.

Wireless Interfaces: If your system has a wireless card, it is usually named wlan0, wlan1, etc.

Loopback Interface: This is a virtual interface named lo that refers to the local system. It is used for communication within the system, without going over the physical network.

Virtual Interfaces: These are software-based interfaces, such as tun0 for VPN connections or docker0 for Docker containers.

How to Identify Specific Network Interfaces

When configuring networking on a Linux server or workstation, it's crucial to know which interfaces correspond to which network connections (e.g., the interface connected to the internet, the internal LAN interface). To identify and manage these interfaces, you need to understand their role in the network:

Internet-facing Interface: This interface, often named eth0, connects the system to the internet or external network. It typically has a public IP address, either static or assigned by DHCP.

Example (for DHCP setup):

auto eth0 iface eth0 inet dhcp

Internal Network Interface: A second interface, such as eth1, is typically used to connect the server to a local network (LAN). This interface usually operates within a private IP address range (e.g., 192.168.1.2 to 192.168.1.255). Devices on the internal network, such as a Windows PC or other devices, can communicate with the server through this interface. The private IP range ensures that these internal devices are not directly accessible from the internet, providing a layer of security.

Example (for static IP setup):

```
auto eth1
iface eth1 inet static
address 192.168.1.1
netmask 255.255.255.0
```

Understanding network interfaces is crucial for network configuration and troubleshooting in Linux. By using commands like ip addr show or ifconfig, you can easily identify which interfaces are active and what their configurations are. Once you have identified the correct interfaces, you can configure them to suit your needs, whether it's for a local area network, internet gateway, or virtual private network. Properly managing and configuring these interfaces allows for reliable communication and network performance.

Networking Configuration Steps

Once you've identified the connected networking devices and determined your IP address (if using a static IP), you can configure /etc/interfaces using a text editor like nano, and add or modify the necessary settings:

For Debian/Ubuntu Systems:

nano /etc/interfaces

If you have a dynamic or changing IP (usually a lower cost internet connection), you should have the following:

 # interfaces(5) file used by ifup(8) and ifdown(8)
 # Please note that this file is written to be used with DHCP, for
 # automatic IP address assignment.

 # See /usr/share/doc/ifupdown/examples/ for more examples.
 # Loopback network interface

```
auto lo
iface lo inet loopback
```

 # Ethernet interface connected to the internet (using DHCP) –
 # Dynamic and Changing IP
```
auto eth0
iface eth0 inet dhcp    # DHCP is set here for changing IP)
```

Explanation

auto lo: The loopback interface, which is always active and used for internal communication within the server.

iface lo inet loopback: The configuration for the loopback interface, ensuring the server can talk to itself.

auto eth0: This line enables the eth0 interface to automatically start on boot.

iface eth0 inet dhcp: This configures the eth0 interface to obtain an IP address automatically using DHCP from the connected network.

If you have a static IP (usually a higher cost internet connection), you should have the following:

 # interfaces(5) file used by ifup(8) and ifdown(8)

 # Please note that this file is configured for a static IP address.

 # Loopback network interface
```
auto lo
iface lo inet loopback
```

 # Ethernet interface with static IP configuration

```
auto eth0
iface eth0 inet static
address 192.168.1.100    # Static IP address
netmask 255.255.255.0    # Subnet mask
gateway 192.168.1.1      # Default gateway (router)
```

 # Google DNS servers (or your local DNS)
```
dns-nameservers 8.8.8.8 8.8.4.4
```

Explanation:

auto lo: Ensures the loopback interface (lo) is always brought up during system startup. The loopback interface is used for internal communication on the server.

iface lo inet loopback: Configures the loopback interface to use the loopback protocol.

auto eth0: Specifies that the eth0 interface should be brought up automatically at boot.

iface eth0 inet static: This sets up eth0 to use a static IP address.

address 192.168.1.100: Your static IP address.

netmask 255.255.255.0: Defines the subnet mask for your local network (this is common for most home networks).

gateway 192.168.1.1: The default gateway, which is typically the IP address 192.168.1.1 that connects the local network to the internet.

dns-nameservers 8.8.8.8 8.8.4.4: This sets the DNS servers to Google's public DNS servers. You can replace these with your local DNS server or other public DNS options.

How to Find Your DNS Servers

To find out what your DNS Nameservers might be, enter the following command:

cat /etc/resolv.conf

You might see something like:

Generated by resolvconf
nameserver 8.8.8.8
nameserver 8.8.4.4

In this case, your system is using Google's public DNS servers. If you see different addresses, such as your local DNS server or your ISP's DNS, you can use those addresses in your /etc/network/interfaces file instead.

If you prefer, you can leave the DNS set to Google's public servers, or replace them with any other preferred DNS servers.

Check with Your ISP:

If you have a static IP provided by your ISP, you can contact them directly to get the DNS server addresses that you should use. They often provide DNS server addresses that are optimal for their network.

For Centos/RedHat Systems:

In CentOS (and other Red Hat-based distributions), the network configuration files are typically located in /etc/sysconfig/network-scripts/. For a DHCP configuration, you would typically edit the file associated with the network interface (e.g., ifcfg-eth0, ifcfg-enp0s3, or another interface name depending on your system). Below is an example of a typical /etc/sysconfig/network-scripts/ifcfg-eth0 file configured for DHCP:

Example of /etc/sysconfig/network-scripts/ifcfg-eth0 for DHCP:

```
# /etc/sysconfig/network-scripts/ifcfg-eth0
DEVICE=eth0
BOOTPROTO=dhcp
ONBOOT=yes
NETBOOT=no
NAME=eth0

# Optional, MAC address of the interface (you can omit # it if not required)
HWADDR=00:11:22:33:44:55
```

Explanation:

DEVICE=eth0: Specifies the network interface name (eth0 in this case, but it could be something else like enp0s3 on newer systems).

BOOTPROTO=dhcp: This indicates that the interface should use DHCP to obtain its IP address automatically.

ONBOOT=yes: This ensures that the interface is brought up automatically at boot time.

NETBOOT=no: This setting is optional and typically used for network boot configurations. In most cases, you can leave it as no.

NAME=eth0: The name of the interface (could also be something like enp0s3 depending on your system).

HWADDR=00:11:22:33:44:55: The MAC address of the network interface (optional, but can be included for reference or static configurations).

Once you've edited or created the configuration file for the interface, you can restart the network service for changes to take effect:

sudo systemctl restart network

Below is an example of a CentOS /etc/sysconfig/network-scripts/ifcfg-eth0 file configured for a static IP address:

Example of /etc/sysconfig/network-scripts/ifcfg-eth0 for Static IP:

```
# /etc/sysconfig/network-scripts/ifcfg-eth0

DEVICE=eth0
BOOTPROTO=static
ONBOOT=yes
NETBOOT=no
NAME=eth0
# Your static IP address
IPADDR=192.168.1.100

NETMASK=255.255.255.0      # The subnet mask

# The gateway IP address (usually your router's IP)
GATEWAY=192.168.1.1

# Primary DNS server (Google's public DNS)
DNS1=8.8.8.8

# Secondary DNS server (Google's public DNS)
DNS2=8.8.4.4
```

Explanation:

DEVICE=eth0: Specifies the network interface name. In this case, eth0, but on newer systems, it could be something like enp0s3 depending on your naming convention.

BOOTPROTO=static: This indicates that the interface should use a static IP configuration instead of DHCP.

ONBOOT=yes: Ensures the interface is brought up automatically when the system boots.

NETBOOT=no: This setting is generally for network boot configurations. It can be left as no.

NAME=eth0: The name of the network interface.

IPADDR=192.168.1.100: Your static IP address.

NETMASK=255.255.255.0: The subnet mask for the network. This is commonly 255.255.255.0 for home networks.

GATEWAY=192.168.1.1: The default gateway IP address, typically your router's IP address.

DNS1=8.8.8.8: The primary DNS server. This example uses Google's public DNS server.

DNS2=8.8.4.4: The secondary DNS server, also using Google's public DNS.

Once you've edited the file with the appropriate details, restart the network service for the changes to take effect:

sudo systemctl restart network

Static vs. Dynamic IP Addresses

A static IP address is a fixed, unchanging IP address assigned to a device. Once assigned, it remains constant unless manually changed. This type of IP address is typically used for devices that need to be consistently reachable, such as servers, routers, or networked printers. It is ideal for scenarios where devices need remote access, such as hosting a website, setting up a VPN, or using remote desktop software. The primary advantage of static IPs is their stability, which ensures that the device can always be accessed at the same address, making it essential for hosting services and businesses requiring reliable remote connections.

Obtaining a static IP address usually involves requesting one from your Internet Service Provider (ISP). However, it often comes at a higher cost than dynamic IP addresses. Additionally, setting up static IPs can be more complex, particularly for those who are not familiar with network configuration. Despite this, static IP addresses are often a necessity for businesses and home networks that require consistent external access.

A dynamic IP address, on the other hand, is assigned to a device automatically by the Dynamic Host Configuration Protocol (DHCP), managed by your ISP. The address assigned can change periodically, depending on the ISP's policies or network configuration. Dynamic IP addresses are best suited for everyday home networks and personal devices that don't require a fixed address. Since the IP address changes each time the device connects to the network, dynamic IPs are typically used for laptops, smartphones, and most household devices, where a consistent address is not necessary.

The benefits of dynamic IP addresses are numerous. They are cheaper than static IP addresses, and because the address is automatically assigned by the network, the setup process is much easier. For most home users, dynamic IP addressing is more than sufficient, as it provides reliable internet access without the need for manual configuration. The downside is that since the IP address can change frequently, it can complicate things like setting up remote access to your network or hosting a server without the help of additional services like Dynamic DNS (DDNS), which allows the use of a domain name that automatically updates to reflect changes in your IP address.

Even with Dynamic DNS (DDNS), it can be challenging to obtain a true Fully Qualified Domain Name (FQDN) for certain services, such as email servers, or other services that require a stable and reliable domain name. DDNS allows you to associate a domain name with a dynamically changing IP address, but the frequent changes in IP address may still cause reliability issues for services that depend on a static, persistent FQDN.

For email servers, in particular, having a fixed, static IP address associated with a domain is often necessary for proper DNS records (such as MX records) and to avoid issues with spam filtering, as many mail providers and servers expect a stable, unchanging IP. However, you can always purchase webmail hosting for your website, ensuring that you have a reliable email service even if you're using a dynamic IP. This allows you to have stable email functionality without needing a static IP address on your own server for your website.

Listed below are some free Dynamic DNS (DDNS) services that you can use:

DuckDNS – A popular free DDNS service that offers simple setup and a subdomain of duckdns.org.
https://www.duckdns.org
No-IP - Offers a free plan with a limited number of domains and requires you to confirm your account every 30 days.

https://www.noip.com

FreeDNS (Afraid.org) - Provides free DDNS with multiple domain options, allowing you to create your own custom subdomains.
https://freedns.afraid.org

Dynu - A free service with unlimited subdomains, and no expiration on the free plan. It also supports both IPv4 and IPv6.
https://www.dynu.com

Cloudflare - While Cloudflare doesn't offer a traditional DDNS service, you can use its DNS management to set up a custom DDNS solution with their API, which can be used to update DNS records automatically.
https://www.cloudflare.com

Static IP addresses are best suited for situations where consistent and reliable remote access is required, such as for web hosting or VPN access, while dynamic IP addresses are ideal for typical home networking, where ease of use and cost-effectiveness are often prioritized.

Configuring a Static IP

To set a static IP of let's say, **192.168.0.100** on both Debian/Ubuntu and CentOS, follow the steps below. Each distribution handles network configuration differently, so I will cover the process for both.

1. Setting a Static IP on Debian/Ubuntu (Using netplan)

For newer versions of Ubuntu (18.04 and later) and Debian that use netplan, follow these steps:

Open a terminal and gain root privileges:

sudo -i

Find your network interface name (e.g., eth0 or ens33) by running:

ip a

Look for the name of the interface you want to configure.

Edit the netplan configuration file:

The configuration file is usually located in /etc/netplan/. It will have a .yaml extension, like 01-netcfg.yaml or something similar.

Open the file for editing:

sudo nano /etc/netplan/01-netcfg.yaml

Modify the configuration file to include the static IP details. Below is an example configuration to set the IP address to **192.168.0.100** with a gateway of **192.168.0.1** and a DNS server of **8.8.8.8**:

```yaml
network:
  version: 2
  renderer: networkd
  ethernets:
    eth0:  # Replace with your actual interface name
      addresses:
        - 192.168.0.100/24
      gateway4: 192.168.0.1
      nameservers:
        addresses:
          - 8.8.8.8
```

Apply the changes:

sudo netplan apply

Verify the changes:

ip a

You should now see **192.168.0.100** assigned to your network interface.

2. Setting a Static IP on CentOS/RHEL (Using nmcli or ifcfg files)

On CentOS 7/8 and RHEL, you can set a static IP using either the NetworkManager CLI (nmcli) or by editing the ifcfg configuration files.

Step-by-Step (using ifcfg files):

Open a terminal and gain root privileges:

sudo -i

Find your network interface name (e.g., eth0 or enp0s3) by running:

ip a

Identify the interface you want to configure.

Edit the network configuration file located in /etc/sysconfig/network-scripts/. The file will be named something like ifcfg-eth0 or ifcfg-enp0s3 based on your interface name.

Open the file for editing:

sudo nano /etc/sysconfig/network-scripts/ifcfg-eth0

Replace "eth0" with your interface name

Modify the file to include your static IP configuration. Here's an example for **192.168.0.100**:

TYPE=Ethernet
BOOTPROTO=none
NAME=eth0 # Replace with your interface name
DEVICE=eth0 # Replace with your interface name

```
ONBOOT=yes
IPADDR=192.168.0.100
PREFIX=24  # This is the netmask (255.255.255.0)
GATEWAY=192.168.0.1
DNS1=8.8.8.8
```

Restart the network service to apply the changes:

sudo systemctl restart NetworkManager

Verify the changes:

ip a

You should now see **192.168.0.100** assigned to your network interface.

Step-by-Step (using nmcli command-line tool):

Open a terminal and gain root privileges:

sudo -i

List your network connections to identify the name of your active network interface:

nmcli connection show

Set the static IP using nmcli:

nmcli connection modify eth0 ipv4.addresses 192.168.0.100/24

nmcli connection modify eth0 ipv4.gateway 192.168.0.1

nmcli connection modify eth0 ipv4.dns 8.8.8.8

nmcli connection modify eth0 ipv4.method manual

Bring the connection down and up to apply the changes:

nmcli connection down eth0

nmcli connection up eth0

Verify the changes:

ip a

The static IP **192.168.0.100** should now be applied to the **eth0** interface.

Configuring Dynamic IP with DHCP

To set up DHCP (Dynamic Host Configuration Protocol) for automatic IP assignment on both Debian/Ubuntu and CentOS, follow these step-by-step guides.

Configuring DHCP on Debian/Ubuntu (Using netplan)

For newer versions of Ubuntu (18.04 and later) and Debian, DHCP is typically handled using netplan.

Open a terminal and gain root privileges:

sudo -i

Find your network interface name (e.g., eth0, ens33) by running:

ip a

Edit the netplan configuration file:

The configuration file is usually located in /etc/netplan/. It will have a .yaml extension (e.g., 01-netcfg.yaml).

Open the file for editing:

sudo nano /etc/netplan/01-netcfg.yaml

Modify the configuration file to use DHCP for automatic IP assignment. Here's an example configuration:

```yaml
network:
version: 2
renderer: networkd
ethernets:
eth0:  # Replace with your actual interface name
dhcp4: yes
```

note: dhcp4: yes enables DHCP for IPv4.

Apply the changes:

sudo netplan apply

Verify the changes:

ip a

You should now see an IP address dynamically assigned to your network interface.

2. Configuring DHCP on CentOS/RHEL (Using ifcfg Files or nmcli)

On CentOS 7/8 and RHEL, you can configure DHCP by editing

the ifcfg files or using nmcli.

Open a terminal and gain root privileges:

sudo -i

Find your network interface name (e.g., eth0 or enp0s3) by running:

ip a

Edit the network configuration file located in /etc/sysconfig/network-scripts/. The file will be named something like ifcfg-eth0 or ifcfg-enp0s3 based on your interface name.

Open the file for editing:

sudo nano /etc/sysconfig/network-scripts/ifcfg-eth0

Replace "eth0" with your interface name

Modify the file to enable DHCP. Here's an example configuration:

TYPE=Ethernet
BOOTPROTO=dhcp
NAME=eth0 # Replace with your actual interface name
DEVICE=eth0 # Replace with your actual interface name
ONBOOT=yes

Note: BOOTPROTO=dhcp ensures that the interface will use DHCP for IP assignment.

Note: ONBOOT=yes ensures that the interface is brought up at boot.

Restart the network service to apply the changes:

sudo systemctl restart NetworkManager

Verify the changes:

ip a

You should now see an IP address dynamically assigned to your network interface.

Step-by-Step (using nmcli command-line tool):

Open a terminal and gain root privileges:

sudo -i

List your network connections to identify the name of your active network interface:

nmcli connection show

Set the connection to use DHCP with nmcli:

nmcli connection modify eth0 ipv4.method auto

Note: auto enables DHCP for automatic IP assignment.

Bring the connection down and up to apply the changes:

nmcli connection down eth0

nmcli connection up eth0

Verify the changes:

ip a

You should now see an IP address dynamically assigned to the eth0 interface.

Special Considerations for Dynamic IP Networks

IP Address Lease and Renewal

DHCP leases are temporary: In a DHCP network, IP addresses are leased to devices for a specific period. Once the lease expires, the client must request to renew the lease or get a new IP. This dynamic nature can cause IP addresses

to change over time unless certain conditions are in place (e.g., DHCP reservation).

Renewal process: If the server fails to renew the lease before it expires, the device could lose network connectivity. Monitoring DHCP lease times and ensuring the lease renewal

is working correctly is important in larger networks.

DHCP Reservations (Static Leases)

If you need certain devices (e.g., servers, printers, or other critical devices) to always receive the same IP address, you should set up DHCP reservations. This ties an IP address to the MAC address of the device, allowing the device to receive the same IP every time it connects to the network.

This is useful for servers (like your Linux server) where you need consistent connectivity or for port forwarding rules.

Handling IP Conflicts

IP conflicts occur when two devices are assigned the same IP address, which can lead to network issues. While DHCP usually prevents conflicts, they can still occur if:

Manual static IPs are set on a device outside of the DHCP scope.

A misconfigured DHCP server assigns an address that's already in use.

To avoid conflicts, ensure your DHCP server has a defined range for IP assignment and manually configure static IP

addresses outside of this range.

DHCP Scope and IP Address Pool

DHCP scope refers to the range of IP addresses that a DHCP server can assign. You need to carefully plan the size of the pool based on the number of devices that will connect to the network.

For example, if you have a small network, you may only need a pool of 192.168.0.100 – 192.168.0.200 for 100 devices. However, for larger networks, the pool should be adjusted accordingly.

Subnet Mask Considerations

The subnet mask defines the range of IP addresses available within the network. For a typical home or small office network using 192.168.x.x, the subnet mask is usually 255.255.255.0 (which allows 254 usable IPs).

For larger networks, you may need to adjust the subnet mask to allow more devices. Make sure that the DHCP server is assigning IP addresses within the correct subnet.

Network Segmentation

In larger or more complex networks, you may need to segment the network into different subnets for performance, security, or management reasons. DHCP can be configured to assign addresses in these subnets by setting up DHCP relays or multiple DHCP scopes.

For instance, having a separate subnet for guest Wi-Fi users and limiting their access to critical internal networks can improve security.

Default Gateway and DNS Assignment

DHCP not only assigns an IP address but also provides clients with additional configuration, including the default gateway (the router's IP) and DNS servers. These values should be correctly configured in the DHCP server to ensure devices can route traffic and resolve domain names.

Incorrect DNS or gateway settings can lead to issues such as devices not being able to connect to the internet or resolve domain names.

Redundancy and Failover

In critical networks, it's common to have multiple DHCP servers for redundancy. This ensures that if one DHCP server fails, another can take over and assign IP addresses.

You can configure DHCP failover with load balancing or hot standby modes. This ensures continuous network operation even if one server goes down.

Security Considerations

DHCP Spoofing: Malicious actors can set up rogue DHCP servers to trick devices into accepting incorrect configurations. This can lead to traffic redirection, man-in-the-middle attacks, or denial of service.

DHCP Snooping: In managed switches, enable DHCP snooping to ensure that only authorized DHCP servers can assign IP addresses to network devices. It prevents rogue DHCP servers from being set up in your network.

DHCP Option Codes

DHCP servers can be configured to send additional options using DHCP option codes. These include things like NTP server addresses, proxy settings, and boot options for devices that require them.

For example, Option 43 can provide custom settings for certain devices like VoIP phones or network printers.

Example DHCP Network Configuration:

For a typical home or small office network with 192.168.0.0/24, consider the following setup:

DHCP Scope: 192.168.0.100 to 192.168.0.200

Gateway: 192.168.0.1 (Router or firewall)

DNS Servers: 8.8.8.8, 8.8.4.4 (Google DNS) or 192.168.0.1 (Router)

Subnet Mask: 255.255.255.0

Lease Time: 24 hours (this can vary based on the number of devices and usage patterns)

Dynamic IP networks provide flexibility by automatically assigning IP addresses, but proper planning is needed to prevent issues like IP conflicts, misconfigurations, and outages. Special considerations include understanding how DHCP leases work, planning your IP range, configuring reservations, and ensuring security against rogue DHCP servers.

Enabling IP Forwarding

IP forwarding is essential for routing traffic between different network interfaces on a Linux server. For example, if your server is acting as a router between two subnets, IP forwarding must be enabled to pass traffic between those subnets.

By default, most Linux distributions have IP forwarding disabled for security reasons. To enable it, you need to modify the system configuration.

Editing the sysctl Configuration

The /etc/sysctl.conf file controls system parameters that influence the kernel's behavior, including IP forwarding. To enable IP forwarding, follow these steps:

Open the sysctl configuration file for editing.
On **Debian/Ubuntu** or **CentOS/RHEL**:

sudo nano /etc/sysctl.conf

Locate the following line in the file:

#net.ipv4.ip_forward = 0

Uncomment the line (remove the #) and change the value to 1 to enable IP forwarding:

net.ipv4.ip_forward = 1

Save and close the file:
In nano, you can press CTRL + O to save and CTRL + X to exit the editor.

Apply the Changes - To apply the changes made in the sysctl.conf file without needing to restart the system, run the following command:

sudo sysctl -p

This command reloads the sysctl configuration and applies the new settings, including enabling IP forwarding.

Verifying IP Forwarding

To verify that IP forwarding has been successfully enabled, you can check the current status by running:
sysctl net.ipv4.ip_forward

If the output is net.ipv4.ip_forward = 1, then IP forwarding is enabled on your system.

Alternatively, you can check the file directly:

cat /proc/sys/net/ipv4/ip_forward

If the result is 1, IP forwarding is enabled. If it is 0, then it is disabled.

Temporary vs. Permanent IP Forwarding

The method above will permanently enable IP forwarding, as changes made in /etc/sysctl.conf persist across reboots. However, you can also enable IP forwarding temporarily without editing the sysctl.conf file:

To temporarily enable IP forwarding until the next reboot, use:

sudo sysctl -w net.ipv4.ip_forward=1
This setting will not persist across reboots. If you restart your system, IP forwarding will be disabled unless it has been configured in /etc/sysctl.conf.

Chapter 4: Implementing Firewall Rules with iptables/ipchains

Introduction to iptables and ipchains

In Linux-based systems, controlling and filtering network traffic is crucial for security, network management, and performance. The tools most commonly used for this purpose are iptables and, in older Linux systems, ipchains. These utilities allow administrators to define rules for handling incoming and outgoing network traffic, effectively acting as a firewall.

What is iptables?

iptables is a user-space utility program used to configure the IP packet filter rules of the Linux kernel. It is part of the Linux netfilter framework, which provides several tools for controlling network traffic. iptables is the most widely used tool for setting up firewalls, performing network address translation (NAT), and configuring packet filtering rules.

It operates at the network layer (Layer 3) and transport layer (Layer 4) of the OSI model, filtering packets based on criteria such as source/destination IP addresses, protocols (TCP, UDP, etc.), ports, and more.

Key Features of iptables:

Packet Filtering: Allows filtering of traffic based on attributes like IP addresses, ports, and protocols.

Network Address Translation (NAT): Used for hiding the internal network from the outside world by altering IP addresses in the packet header.

Stateful Packet Inspection: Tracks the state of connections, allowing or denying packets based on the connection state (e.g., established, related).

Logging: Provides logging capabilities for monitoring network activity.

Example Commands:

List all rules:

```
sudo iptables -L
```

Allow incoming HTTP traffic:

```
sudo iptables -A INPUT -p tcp --dport 80 -j ACCEPT
```

Block all incoming traffic except for SSH:

```
sudo iptables -A INPUT -p tcp --dport 22 -j ACCEPT
sudo iptables -A INPUT -j DROP
```

What is ipchains?

ipchains was the predecessor to iptables and was used in older Linux distributions (before kernel version 2.4). While iptables is now the standard tool for firewall configuration, ipchains was widely used for packet filtering and firewall management before being replaced.

ipchains operated in a similar manner to iptables, but it lacked some of the features that iptables introduced, such as **stateful packet inspection** and more granular control over NAT.

ipchains was structured to operate with **chains** and **rules** in much the same way as iptables, but it was less flexible and didn't provide the same level of control over network traffic.

Example Commands:

List current rules:

sudo ipchains -L

Allow HTTP traffic:

sudo ipchains -A input -p tcp -s 0/0 80 -j ACCEPT

Block all incoming traffic:

sudo ipchains -A input -j DENY

Differences Between iptables and ipchains

Feature	iptables	ipchains
Kernel Version	Used in Linux 2.4.x and newer kernels	Used in older Linux 2.2.x kernels
Stateful Inspection	Yes, tracks connection states (e.g., NEW, ESTABLISHED)	No, simple packet filtering only
NAT Support	Full support for NAT and masquerading	Limited NAT support
Flexibility	Highly flexible with advanced filtering options	Basic filtering rules, limited customization
Performance	More efficient with more features	Less efficient, fewer features

When to Use iptables vs. ipchains

Use iptables: If you're using a modern Linux kernel (2.4 or later), iptables is the recommended tool. It is more powerful and provides better performance, especially for managing complex firewalls, NAT configurations, and stateful packet filtering.

Use ipchains: Only if you're working with legacy systems or older distributions that still rely on ipchains. For most use cases today, iptables should be the tool of choice.

Transitioning from ipchains to iptables

For administrators working with legacy systems,

transitioning from ipchains to iptables is recommended. The transition is not overly complex, as many of the concepts are similar. The main differences are in the syntax and added features like stateful inspection, which enhance security and flexibility.

iptables has largely replaced ipchains in modern Linux distributions due to its enhanced features, greater flexibility, and better security capabilities. While ipchains is still found in older systems, it is highly recommended to switch to iptables for more robust firewall and network traffic management. Understanding both tools provides valuable historical context and ensures that systems running older kernels can still be secured effectively.

Installing iptables on Debian/Ubuntu and CentOS

iptables is typically pre-installed on most modern Linux distributions, but if it is not installed, you can easily install it using the package manager. Additionally, to ensure iptables rules persist across reboots, you'll need to save the rules and ensure they are reloaded when the system starts up.

Installing iptables on Debian/Ubuntu

Check if iptables is already installed.

To verify if iptables is already installed, you can run the following command:

sudo iptables –version

If it's not installed, you'll get an error message, and you can proceed with the installation steps.

Use the following command to install iptables:

sudo apt update

sudo apt install iptables

Ensure iptables rules persist after reboot:

By default, iptables rules are lost after a reboot. To make sure they are persistent, you need to save the rules to a file and restore them at boot.

Install the iptables-persistent package, which automatically saves and restores iptables rules:

sudo apt install iptables-persistent

During installation, you will be prompted to save the current iptables rules. Choose Yes to save the rules.

If you make changes to your firewall rules, you can manually save them using:

sudo netfilter-persistent save

To load the rules on boot, the iptables-persistent package takes care of that automatically by using systemd.

Verify that the rules are persistent:

After rebooting your system, verify that the rules have been reloaded:

sudo iptables -L

Installing iptables on CentOS

Check if iptables is installed.

Run the following command to check if iptables is installed:

sudo iptables --version

If iptables is not installed, proceed with the following steps to install it.

To install iptables, use the yum package manager:

sudo yum install iptables

If you're using CentOS 8 or newer, you may need to use dnf instead:

sudo dnf install iptables

Ensure iptables rules persist after reboot:

On CentOS, you will need to ensure that iptables rules are saved and restored after reboot. CentOS provides a service that can save the rules.

To save the current rules:

sudo service iptables save

This saves the current firewall rules to the file /etc/sysconfig/iptables.

To enable iptables to restore the saved rules on boot, use:

sudo systemctl enable iptables

If you're using CentOS 8 or newer (with firewalld), you may need to disable firewalld and enable iptables manually:

sudo systemctl stop firewalld

sudo systemctl disable firewalld

sudo systemctl enable iptables

sudo systemctl start iptables

Verify that the rules are persistent:

After rebooting the system, you can verify that the rules have been restored:

sudo iptables -L

This will list the current rules that are active after the system has rebooted.

Introduction to NAT (Network Address Translation)

Network Address Translation (NAT) is a technique used in networking that allows multiple devices on a private network to share a single public IP address when accessing the internet. NAT is primarily used for three purposes:

Conserving public IP addresses: By allowing multiple devices to use a single public IP address, NAT helps in mitigating the shortage of IPv4 addresses.

Enhancing security: By masking the internal private IP addresses of devices behind a single public IP address, NAT helps protect the devices from direct access from the internet, providing an additional layer of security.

Enabling routing flexibility: NAT allows organizations to set up private networks with arbitrary IP addresses that do not conflict with public address spaces, and still be able to communicate with the wider internet.

NAT works by modifying the source or destination IP addresses in the packet headers as they pass through a router or firewall. This is particularly useful in scenarios where private networks (using IP addresses in the reserved ranges like 192.168.x.x, 10.x.x.x, 172.16.x.x to 172.31.x.x) need to communicate over the public internet.

How NAT Works in Routing and Firewall Scenarios

In a typical network setup, devices within a private network communicate with each other using private IP addresses. These devices are behind a router or firewall that connects the private network to the public internet. When a device within the private network needs to access a remote server (such as browsing a website), it sends a packet to the router.

Outbound Traffic (Private to Public):

The device in the private network sends a request (such as an HTTP request to access a website).

The router receives the request and modifies the source IP address of the outgoing packet, replacing the private IP address (e.g., 192.168.1.2) with the router's public IP address.

The router also keeps a translation table that records the mapping between the internal private IP and port to the external public IP and port.

The request is sent to the public internet with the public IP address of the router.

When the response is received from the destination server (e.g., the website), the router uses the translation table to forward the packet to the correct internal device.

Inbound Traffic (Public to Private):

If an inbound request (e.g., from a public server) arrives at the router, the router checks its NAT translation table to see if the request corresponds to a valid session initiated by a device inside the network.

The router forwards the packet to the internal device that initiated the session, using the private IP address and port.

In cases where the NAT device is set up for port forwarding (such as when hosting a web server), the router can be configured to forward traffic from a specific public port to an internal device's private IP address.

This mechanism allows multiple devices on a private network to access the internet using one public IP address, and also shields internal devices from direct access, enhancing security.

Masquerading for Dynamic IP Setups

In many cases, an internet connection will use a dynamic IP address, which means the public IP address of the router can change periodically (for example, every time the router reconnects to the ISP). This is common with most home or small office setups, where the ISP assigns a dynamic public IP address to the router.

Masquerading is a special form of NAT often used in dynamic IP setups to handle this scenario. It allows a router to automatically translate private IP addresses into the router's dynamic public IP address, without requiring manual intervention.

Here's how masquerading works in a dynamic IP setup:

Router Setup:

When a device on the private network sends a request to access the internet, the router (acting as a NAT gateway) automatically modifies the packet's source address to its public IP.

Since the public IP address is dynamic, the router doesn't need to keep track of a fixed IP. It uses its current public IP address for outgoing traffic, and masquerades the internal device's IP address.

Handling Dynamic IP Changes:

When the router's public IP changes (due to the dynamic

nature of the ISP's connection), masquerading ensures that the translation of private IP addresses to the new public IP address is handled automatically.

This is important because the router does not have to

maintain any static mappings for the internal devices to the external IP address, making it seamless for the internal network to continue communicating with external servers.

Configuring Masquerading in Linux with iptables

In Linux, masquerading can be easily set up using the iptables firewall. Here's how you can configure it:

Enable IP forwarding (if not already enabled): First, ensure that IP forwarding is enabled on the system, allowing it to route traffic between interfaces:

sudo sysctl -w net.ipv4.ip_forward=1

To make this change persistent across reboots, edit /etc/sysctl.conf:

sudo nano /etc/sysctl.conf

Find the line that says #net.ipv4.ip_forward=1 and uncomment it by removing the # at the beginning of the line. Then save and close the file. Apply the changes with:

sudo sysctl -p

Set up NAT masquerading: Add the following rule to iptables to enable masquerading for outgoing traffic:

```
sudo iptables -t nat -A POSTROUTING -o eth0 -j MASQUERADE
```

eth0 is the network interface connected to the public internet. Make sure you replace it with the correct interface name for your system.

Save the iptables rules: To make the rules persistent after reboot, you need to save them. On Debian-based systems, you can use iptables-persistent:

```
sudo apt install iptables-persistent
```

On CentOS/RHEL systems, you can save the rules like this:

```
sudo service iptables save
```

NAT and masquerading are powerful tools for managing IP addresses and enhancing security in network setups. NAT allows private networks to communicate with the outside world using a single public IP address, and masquerading is particularly useful when the public IP address is dynamic, as

it enables seamless network communication without needing to update configurations every time the public IP changes. These techniques are often employed in home networks, small office setups, and virtual private networks (VPNs), and are critical for the proper functioning of most modern networks.

Basic Firewall Rules with iptables

A firewall is a critical component in securing a network by controlling incoming and outgoing traffic based on predefined rules. In Linux systems, iptables is the tool most commonly used to configure firewall rules. It allows users to filter and control network traffic, blocking unwanted connections while permitting necessary services to function.

Here, we will cover some of the basic firewall rules that can be set using iptables, including how to drop unwanted traffic, allow essential traffic like HTTP and DNS, perform port forwarding, open ports for services like SSH and HTTP, and prevent common attacks.

Dropping Unwanted Traffic

One of the first steps in setting up a firewall is to deny all traffic by default and then selectively allow traffic for services you wish to use. This ensures that only the necessary and trusted services can communicate through your firewall.

Default Policy to Drop Traffic

You can start by setting the default policy for each chain (INPUT, OUTPUT, FORWARD) to DROP. This means that, by default, no traffic will be allowed to pass through the firewall unless explicitly permitted by a rule.

sudo iptables -P INPUT DROP

sudo iptables -P FORWARD DROP

sudo iptables -P OUTPUT ACCEPT

INPUT: Controls inbound traffic (traffic entering the server).

FORWARD: Controls traffic being forwarded through the server (typically used in routing scenarios).

OUTPUT: Controls outbound traffic (traffic leaving the server).

Setting the default INPUT and FORWARD chains to DROP ensures that any traffic not explicitly allowed by other rules will be blocked, while allowing all outgoing traffic by default (since the server itself is typically making requests).

Allowing Essential Traffic

After dropping all traffic by default, you need to allow traffic for essential services like HTTP, HTTPS, DNS, and SSH. You can create rules to accept traffic on specific ports for these services.

Allowing HTTP (Port 80) and HTTPS (Port 443)

These are the default ports for web traffic. If your server is hosting a website, you'll need to allow traffic on these ports.

```
# Allow HTTP traffic
sudo iptables -A INPUT -p tcp --dport 80 -j ACCEPT

# Allow HTTPS traffic
sudo iptables -A INPUT -p tcp --dport 443 -j ACCEPT
```

Allowing DNS (Port 53)

If your server needs to resolve domain names, you must allow DNS queries (which usually occur on port 53).

Allow DNS queries
```
sudo iptables -A INPUT -p udp --dport 53 -j ACCEPT
```

Allowing SSH (Port 22)

For remote administration of your server, you will typically use SSH. By default, SSH uses port 22, so you will need to allow traffic on this port.

Allow SSH traffic
```
sudo iptables -A INPUT -p tcp --dport 22 -j ACCEPT
```

Port Forwarding and Opening Ports for Services

Port forwarding allows incoming traffic on specific ports to be forwarded to a local service or device in the network. For example, if you want to allow external users to connect to a web server running on your internal network, you can

configure port forwarding.

Example: Port Forwarding for HTTP Traffic

To forward incoming HTTP traffic (port 80) to an internal server with IP address 192.168.1.2, you can use the following rule:

```
sudo iptables -t nat -A PREROUTING -p tcp --dport 80 -j DNAT --to-destination 192.168.1.2:80
```

This rule tells the firewall to forward any incoming traffic on port 80 to the internal server at 192.168.1.2.

Example: Opening Ports for a Service (FTP, HTTP)

To open ports for services such as FTP (port 21) or custom applications, you can add rules similar to the following:

```
# Allow FTP
sudo iptables -A INPUT -p tcp --dport 21 -j ACCEPT

ACCEPT  # Allow HTTP on port 8080
sudo iptables -A INPUT -p tcp --dport 8080 -j
```

These rules allow incoming FTP traffic and HTTP traffic on port 8080, respectively.

Preventing Common Attacks

A key role of a firewall is to prevent attacks that could compromise the security of the server or network. Here, we

will cover two common types of attacks and how to mitigate them using iptables: SYN floods and port scanning.

Preventing SYN Flood Attacks

A SYN flood is a type of Denial-of-Service (DoS) attack where an attacker sends a large number of SYN requests to a server, without completing the handshake, causing the server to become overwhelmed and potentially crash.

To mitigate SYN flood attacks, you can use the following iptables rule to limit the number of half-open connections:

```
sudo iptables -A INPUT -p tcp --syn -m limit --limit 1/s -j ACCEPT
```

This rule ensures that only one new incoming connection request per second is allowed, which helps protect the server from SYN flood attacks.

Preventing Port Scanning

Port scanning is a technique used by attackers to discover open ports on a server, which can then be exploited. To detect and prevent basic port scans, you can use iptables to drop incoming packets that exhibit suspicious patterns (e.g., a large number of connections from the same IP).

You can block connections that attempt to open too many connections in a short period of time:

```
sudo iptables -A INPUT -p tcp --syn -m limit --limit 10/s --limit-burst 20 -j ACCEPT
```

This rule limits the number of new SYN packets from the same source IP address, making it more difficult for attackers to scan the server quickly.

Another technique is to drop packets from IP addresses that are attempting to perform suspicious behaviors:

```
sudo iptables -A INPUT -p tcp --dport 1:1024 -m recent --set --name portscan

sudo iptables -A INPUT -p tcp --dport 1:1024 -m recent --update --seconds 60 --hitcount 5 -j DROP
```

This rule helps block IP addresses that attempt to scan more than five ports within 60 seconds, which is characteristic of port scanning.

By using iptables, you can create a powerful firewall to protect your Linux server from unwanted traffic and attacks. Key strategies include:

Dropping all traffic by default and then selectively allowing traffic for services such as HTTP, DNS, and SSH.

Port forwarding and opening specific ports to allow inbound connections to services behind the firewall.

Mitigating common attacks like SYN floods and port scanning by applying appropriate rules.

When configuring your firewall, always ensure that essential services are accessible while minimizing your exposure to potential threats.

Protecting Against Brute-Force Attacks

Fail2Ban is a popular security tool that helps protect your server from brute-force attacks by monitoring log files for suspicious activity and automatically blocking malicious IP addresses. It works by scanning log files for repeated failed login attempts, identifying the source IP addresses responsible for these attempts, and then using firewall rules (such as iptables) to block these IPs temporarily.

In this section, guides you through installing and configuring Fail2Ban on both Debian/Ubuntu and CentOS, and explain how it helps safeguard your server against brute-force attacks.

What is Fail2Ban?

Fail2Ban is a tool that actively monitors log files for specific patterns of failed login attempts or other suspicious activity, such as port scanning, and blocks offending IP addresses. By temporarily blocking malicious IP addresses using firewall rules, Fail2Ban prevents attackers from continuing their brute-force attempts. This is especially useful for services like SSH, FTP, HTTP, and other common server applications.

Installing Fail2Ban

Debian/Ubuntu

Step 1: Install Fail2Ban

Update your package list and install Fail2Ban with the following commands:

sudo apt update

sudo apt install fail2ban

This will install the Fail2Ban package and the necessary dependencies.

Step 2: Start and Enable Fail2Ban

Once installed, you can start Fail2Ban and enable it to start automatically on boot:

sudo systemctl start fail2ban

sudo systemctl enable fail2ban

To verify that Fail2Ban is running, use:

sudo systemctl status fail2ban

CentOS/RHEL

On CentOS and other Red Hat-based systems, you can install Fail2Ban using the yum or dnf package manager.

Step 1: Install Fail2Ban

sudo yum install epel-release   # Enable the EPEL repository (if not already enabled)

sudo yum install fail2ban

For CentOS 8 and later, you can use dnf:

sudo dnf install fail2ban

Step 2: Start and Enable Fail2Ban

Start the Fail2Ban service and enable it to start automatically at boot:

sudo systemctl start fail2ban

sudo systemctl enable fail2ban

Verify that Fail2Ban is active:

sudo systemctl status fail2ban

Configuring Fail2Ban

Fail2Ban comes with default configurations that work out of the box for many common services, such as SSH, but you can customize it further by editing its configuration files.

Understanding Fail2Ban Configuration Files

The main configuration files for Fail2Ban are:

/etc/fail2ban/jail.conf: This is the default configuration file, which contains the settings for different services.

/etc/fail2ban/jail.local: This file is where you should make custom configurations to override the default settings in jail.conf. It's recommended to use jail.local to avoid overwriting settings during updates.

Basic Configuration Steps

Step 1: Create or Edit jail.local

If jail.local does not already exist, you should create it by copying the default configuration file (jail.conf):

sudo cp /etc/fail2ban/jail.conf /etc/fail2ban/jail.local

Now, open the jail.local file to customize the configuration:

sudo nano /etc/fail2ban/jail.local

Step 2: Configure SSH Protection

Fail2Ban is often used to protect SSH from brute-force login attempts. In the [sshd] section of jail.local, you can configure Fail2Ban to monitor SSH login attempts.

Locate the [sshd] section and make sure it is enabled. You can also set the parameters for banning:

```
[sshd]
enabled = true
port = ssh
filter = sshd
logpath = /var/log/auth.log
maxretry = 3
bantime = 600
findtime = 600
```

Explanation:

enabled = true: Enables protection for SSH.

port = ssh: Specifies the port to monitor (default is port 22).

filter = sshd: Defines which filter to use for parsing the log file.

logpath = /var/log/auth.log: Specifies the log file to monitor for failed login attempts (this path might differ, especially on CentOS, where it's usually /var/log/secure).

maxretry = 3: The number of failed login attempts allowed before banning the IP.

bantime = 600: The duration (in seconds) that the offending IP address will be blocked (here, 10 minutes).

findtime = 600: The time window (in seconds) in which the failed login attempts are counted.

Step 3: Configure General Settings (Optional)

You can adjust general settings such as the ignoreip option, which specifies IP addresses or ranges that should never be blocked (e.g., your own trusted network or VPN). This can be added at the top of the jail.local file:

ignoreip = 127.0.0.1/8 ::1

You can also specify other services you want to protect (like FTP, HTTP, etc.) by finding and modifying their respective sections (e.g., [vsftpd], [apache]).

Step 4: Restart Fail2Ban

Once you've configured Fail2Ban, restart the service to apply the changes:

sudo systemctl restart fail2ban

4. Verifying Fail2Ban Status

To check if Fail2Ban is correctly blocking malicious IP addresses, use the following command:

sudo fail2ban-client status

This command shows the status of Fail2Ban and which jails (services) are being monitored. To see details about a specific jail (e.g., SSH), use:

sudo fail2ban-client status sshd

This will display information about banned IPs, the number of failed attempts, and the ban duration.

5. Viewing Banned IP Addresses

To see which IPs have been banned by Fail2Ban, use the following command:

sudo iptables -L

Fail2Ban uses iptables to block offending IP addresses, so you can inspect the output of iptables to see the active bans.

Alternatively, you can list the bans using:

sudo fail2ban-client get sshd banned

6. Unbanning an IP Address

If you want to manually unban an IP address, use the following command:

sudo fail2ban-client set sshd unbanip <IP_ADDRESS>

Replace <IP_ADDRESS> with the IP you wish to unban.

Fail2Ban is a powerful tool for protecting your server from brute-force and other malicious attacks by blocking suspicious IP addresses. After installing and configuring Fail2Ban on Debian/Ubuntu or CentOS, you can easily customize the service to monitor various applications (e.g., SSH, FTP, HTTP) and take action against repeated failed login attempts. With its automated banning mechanism, Fail2Ban can significantly enhance the security of your system without requiring constant manual intervention.

Advanced iptables Rules: Enhancing Network Security

iptables is a powerful Linux tool for managing network traffic. It allows administrators to create rules to filter traffic, control access to services, and prevent unauthorized access. In this section, we will explore advanced iptables rules that help to further enhance network security. Specifically, we will cover rate limiting to prevent abuse of network resources and the use of IP blacklists and whitelists to control access to your system based on IP addresses.

Configuring Rate Limiting

Rate limiting is a technique used to control the amount of traffic that can pass through a network interface or a specific service. It is particularly useful for preventing DoS (Denial of Service) or brute-force attacks, where an attacker tries to overload the system with excessive requests in a short period of time.

Basic Rate Limiting

You can configure rate limiting in iptables to limit the number of connections a specific IP can make to a service within a certain time frame. The following example demonstrates how to set up rate limiting for incoming SSH connections:

```
sudo iptables -A INPUT -p tcp --dport 22 -i eth0 -m limit --limit 3/minute
--limit-burst 6 -j ACCEPT
```

Explanation:

-A INPUT: Appends the rule to the INPUT chain, which handles incoming traffic.

-p tcp: Specifies that the rule applies to TCP packets.

--dport 22: The destination port, in this case, SSH (port 22).

-i eth0: The interface through which the packets are received (replace eth0 with your interface name).

-m limit: Uses the limit module to control the rate of incoming connections.

--limit 3/minute: Allows only 3 connections per minute from a single IP address.

--limit-burst 6: Allows an initial burst of 6 connections, then enforces the limit.

-j ACCEPT: If the traffic matches the rule, it will be accepted.

Rate Limiting for SYN Floods

SYN floods are a type of DoS attack where an attacker sends a large number of TCP SYN requests to a target system. You can use rate limiting to mitigate this type of attack. The following command limits the number of SYN packets:

```
sudo iptables -A INPUT -p tcp --syn -m limit --limit 1/s --limit-burst 3 -j ACCEPT
```

Explanation:

--syn: Matches only TCP packets with the SYN flag set, which are used to initiate a connection.

--limit 1/s: Limits the incoming SYN packets to 1 per second.

--limit-burst 3: Allows an initial burst of up to 3 SYN packets before rate limiting applies.

-j ACCEPT: Accepts the traffic that matches the rule.

Dropping Excessive Traffic

If an IP address exceeds the specified rate limit, you may want to drop excess traffic rather than allowing it. For example, you can block further SSH attempts after the rate limit is reached:

```
sudo iptables -A INPUT -p tcp --dport 22 -i eth0 -m limit --limit 3/minute
--limit-burst 6 -j ACCEPT
```

```
sudo iptables -A INPUT -p tcp --dport 22 -i eth0 -j DROP
```

The first rule allows the first 3 connections per minute, and the second rule drops any additional SSH traffic after the rate limit is exceeded.

IP Blacklists and Whitelists

IP blacklists are used to block traffic from known malicious or unwanted IP addresses, while whitelists ensure that trusted IP addresses are always allowed access to the server.

IP Blacklist

You can block an IP address using iptables by adding a rule that drops all incoming traffic from that specific IP. For example, to block the IP 192.168.1.100, use the following command:

sudo iptables -A INPUT -s 192.168.1.100 -j DROP

Explanation:

-A INPUT: Adds a rule to the INPUT chain, which handles incoming traffic.

-s 192.168.1.100: Specifies the source IP address to block.

-j DROP: Drops the traffic from the specified IP address.

You can also block an entire range of IPs by specifying a subnet. For example, to block all IP addresses in the 192.168.1.0/24 network:

sudo iptables -A INPUT -s 192.168.1.0/24 -j DROP

This will block all incoming traffic from any IP within the 192.168.1.0 subnet.

IP Whitelist

An IP whitelist ensures that only certain trusted IP addresses are allowed to connect to your server. For example, to allow only the IP 192.168.1.100 to access SSH, while blocking all others, you would set up the following rules:

```
sudo iptables -A INPUT -p tcp --dport 22 -s 192.168.1.100 -j ACCEPT
sudo iptables -A INPUT -p tcp --dport 22 -j DROP
```

Explanation:

The first rule allows incoming SSH traffic only from 192.168.1.100.

The second rule blocks all other incoming SSH traffic.

You can also apply whitelisting to other services, such as HTTP (port 80) or HTTPS (port 443), by replacing the --dport 22 with the appropriate port numbers.

Dynamic Blacklist/Whitelist Using a File

For managing large sets of blacklisted or whitelisted IPs, you can dynamically load IPs from a file using a loop. For example, if you have a file named blacklist.txt that contains a list of IPs to block, you can execute the following script to apply the rules:

```
for ip in $(cat /path/to/blacklist.txt); do
```

```
sudo iptables -A INPUT -s $ip -j DROP
```

```
done
```

This script will read the IP addresses from blacklist.txt and add a DROP rule for each IP in the list.

Similarly, to whitelist a list of IPs:

```
for ip in $(cat /path/to/whitelist.txt); do
```

```
sudo iptables -A INPUT -s $ip -j ACCEPT
```

```
done
```

Combining Blacklists, Whitelists, and Rate Limiting

By combining rate limiting with IP blacklists and whitelists, you can create a more secure system. For example, you could block traffic from certain countries, rate limit others, and allow trusted users to connect freely.

Here's an example configuration that allows trusted users to connect without restriction, blocks known bad IPs, and rate limits everyone else:

```
# Allow trusted IPs (whitelist)
```

```
sudo iptables -A INPUT -s 192.168.1.100 -j ACCEPT
```

```
# Block malicious IPs (blacklist)
```

```
sudo iptables -A INPUT -s 203.0.113.10 -j DROP
```

Rate limit other connections (except for trusted IPs)

```
sudo iptables -A INPUT -p tcp --dport 22 -m limit --limit 3/minute --limit-burst 6 -j ACCEPT
```

```
sudo iptables -A INPUT -p tcp --dport 22 -j DROP
```

This configuration ensures that only trusted IP addresses can connect without limits, malicious IP addresses are blocked, and all other IP addresses are rate-limited to prevent abuse.

Advanced iptables rules such as rate limiting, IP blacklists, and whitelists offer powerful tools to enhance your network's security. Rate limiting helps prevent abuse by limiting the number of connections from a single source, IP blacklists allow you to block known malicious sources, and whitelists ensure that trusted IPs always have access. By combining these techniques, you can create a highly secure network environment that protects against various types of attacks and misuse.

Chapter 5: Dynamic IP Setup with DDNS

In many home or small office networks, Internet Service Providers (ISPs) assign dynamic IP addresses to their customers. A dynamic IP address means that the address assigned to your router or gateway can change periodically, which can create challenges when trying to access your network remotely. Dynamic DNS (DDNS) is a solution to this problem, providing a way to link a domain name to a dynamic IP address, ensuring that external access remains consistent even as the IP address changes.

Understanding Dynamic DNS (DDNS)

Dynamic DNS (DDNS) is a service that automatically updates the DNS records of a domain whenever the public IP address of a device (such as a router or server) changes. This is particularly useful for home users or small businesses that do not have a static IP from their ISP but still need to make services like remote desktop, web hosting, or file sharing accessible from the outside world.

What is DDNS?

DDNS stands for Dynamic Domain Name System. Traditional DNS is used to map domain names (like example.com) to static IP addresses (like 192.0.2.1). However, in a typical home network, the public IP address assigned to your router is not static—it changes periodically, typically whenever the router is rebooted or the ISP reassigns the IP address.

With DDNS, when your router's public IP changes, a DDNS client running on the router or a connected device automatically updates the DNS records of your domain with the new IP address. This allows anyone trying to reach your domain to always be directed to the correct IP address, even if it changes frequently.

Why is DDNS Essential for Home Networks with Dynamic IPs?

Accessing Devices Remotely: If you host a service (e.g., a web server, security camera, game server) in your home network, you may want to access it remotely. However, with a dynamic IP, your router's IP address changes from time to time, which can break the connection if someone tries to access it using the old IP address.

Consistency: By using DDNS, you can associate a domain name (like home.example.com) with your home network's dynamic IP. Even if the IP address changes, DDNS ensures the domain name always points to the correct IP, so you can continue to access your network seamlessly without needing to keep track of the changing IP.

Cost-Effective: Instead of paying for a static IP from your ISP (which can be more expensive), DDNS allows you to use a dynamic IP and still have the same benefits of external access via a fixed domain name. This makes it a cost-effective solution for home users and small businesses.

How DDNS Works

Here's how DDNS works in a typical home network setup:

Router/Device with DDNS Client: You need a device (usually your router or a server) that supports DDNS and has a DDNS client installed. Many modern routers have DDNS functionality built in, and you can configure them via their web interface.

DDNS Provider: To use DDNS, you must register with a DDNS service provider. These providers typically offer free or paid services, with popular providers such as No-IP, DynDNS, and DuckDNS. When you register, you will receive a subdomain (e.g., yourname.dyndns.org) that will be linked to your dynamic IP address.

IP Address Update: When your router's IP address changes (due to an ISP change or reboot), the DDNS client detects the change and sends an update to the DDNS service provider, informing them of the new IP address.

DNS Resolution: The DDNS service provider updates the DNS records associated with your domain or subdomain. As a result, when someone types in your domain name (e.g., home.example.com), the DNS request is resolved to the updated IP address.

Setting Up DDNS for a Home Network

Sign Up for a DDNS Service: Choose a DDNS provider and sign up for an account. After registering, you will be given a subdomain and credentials for configuring your router or device. For example, with **No-IP**, you might get a domain like homeexample.no-ip.org.

Configure DDNS in Your Router:

Log in to your router's web interface.

Look for a section related to DDNS, which may be under settings like Network, WAN, or Dynamic DNS.

Enter the DDNS provider details (e.g., your username, password, and the subdomain you created).

Save the settings and apply them.

Test the DDNS Configuration:

After configuring DDNS, disconnect and reconnect your router to trigger an IP address change (if necessary).

Check if the domain (homeexample.no-ip.org) resolves to the correct public IP by using a DNS lookup tool like nslookup or dig, or simply by typing the domain name in your browser.

Try accessing the service you've set up at home (e.g., a web server or SSH) using the domain name to ensure everything works as expected.

Keep the DDNS Client Running: Some routers automatically update the DDNS provider whenever the IP changes, while others may require a DDNS client application running on a computer or server in your network. If your router does not support DDNS, or if you want more control, you can install the DDNS client software on a computer or Raspberry Pi that will update the DDNS provider when the IP changes.

Masquerading for Dynamic IP Setups

If you are using a dynamic IP with a router and need to access your home network remotely (e.g., SSH, remote desktop, or a home server), you may also want to set up NAT (Network Address Translation) or masquerading on your router to allow internal devices to communicate with the outside world without exposing your private IPs directly.

Masquerading allows internal devices (with private IPs) to share the router's public IP address for outbound connections. This is commonly used in dynamic IP scenarios where the router's public IP changes frequently.

DDNS (Dynamic DNS) is an invaluable tool for home networks that use dynamic IP addresses from their ISP. It allows you to associate a domain name with a dynamic IP, ensuring reliable external access to your services, even when your IP address changes. Setting up DDNS is relatively simple and can be done with minimal cost, making it ideal for home users, small businesses, or anyone who requires remote access to their network. By integrating DDNS with masquerading, you can maintain consistent and secure access to your home network's services, no matter how often your public IP address changes.

Installing and Configuring DDNS Client

Dynamic DNS (DDNS) allows you to associate a domain name with your changing public IP address, which is crucial for accessing your server remotely, especially if you're using a dynamic IP from your ISP. Below is a step-by-step guide on how to install and configure a DDNS client (such as ddclient) on Debian/Ubuntu and CentOS systems to automatically update the DNS records whenever your IP address changes.

Debian/Ubuntu: Using ddclient

Step 1: Install ddclient

ddclient is a popular DDNS client that can update DNS records for various DDNS services.

Update your package list and install ddclient:

sudo apt update

sudo apt install ddclient

During the installation process, you will be prompted to configure ddclient. You can select your DDNS provider and configure settings for automatic updates. However, you can skip this and configure it manually later if necessary.

Step 2: Configure ddclient

The main configuration file for ddclient is located at /etc/ddclient.conf.

Open the configuration file in a text editor:

sudo nano /etc/ddclient.conf

Edit the configuration file with the following details:

DDNS provider: This is the DDNS service you're using (e.g., No-IP, DynDNS, DuckDNS).

Username: Your DDNS account's username.

Password: Your DDNS account's password or API key.

Domain: The subdomain you want to update.

Example configuration for **No-IP**:

protocol=noip

use=web, web=checkip.dyndns.com

server=dynupdate.no-ip.com

login=your-username

password='your-password'

yourdomain.no-ip.org

Save and exit the file (Ctrl + X, then Y to confirm).

Step 3: Automate IP Updates with Cron

To keep your DNS record up-to-date, you need to run ddclient periodically. We'll use **cron** to automate this process.

Edit the crontab for ddclient:

sudo crontab -e

Add the following line to run ddclient every 5 minutes:

*/5 * * * * /usr/sbin/ddclient -daemon 300 -syslog

This cron job will run ddclient every 5 minutes (300 seconds), ensuring your DDNS provider is updated with the correct IP address.

Save and exit the crontab editor.

Step 4: Verify the DDNS Update

To check if ddclient is updating your IP address correctly, you can use dig or nslookup to query the DNS records for your domain.

Use dig to verify the current IP address associated with your DDNS domain:

dig yourdomain.no-ip.org

Alternatively, use nslookup:

nslookup yourdomain.no-ip.org

These commands should show your current public IP address. If everything is set up correctly, it should match your current dynamic IP.

CentOS: Installing and Configuring ddclient or Similar Tools

On CentOS, we can use the ddclient package or a similar tool like inadyn to manage DDNS updates.

Step 1: Install ddclient

First, install ddclient from the EPEL (Extra Packages for Enterprise Linux) repository:

sudo yum install epel-release

sudo yum install ddclient

Configure ddclient in a similar way as on Debian/Ubuntu, by editing the /etc/ddclient.conf file.

Step 2: Configure ddclient

Open the ddclient configuration file:

sudo nano /etc/ddclient.conf

Add the necessary configuration for your DDNS provider (similar to the Debian/Ubuntu steps).

Example for **No-IP**:

protocol=noip

use=web, web=checkip.dyndns.com

server=dynupdate.no-ip.com

login=your-username

password='your-password'

yourdomain.no-ip.org

Save the file and exit the editor.

Step 3: Automate DDNS Updates with Cron

As with Debian/Ubuntu, you will use cron to automate the updates.

Edit the crontab for ddclient:

sudo crontab -e

Add the following line to run ddclient every 5 minutes:

*/5 * * * * /usr/sbin/ddclient -daemon 300 -syslog

Save and exit the crontab editor.

Step 4: Verify the DDNS Update

You can use the dig or nslookup commands to verify that your DDNS updates are working correctly, just as shown in the Debian/Ubuntu setup.

Configuring Your DDNS Provider

After installing and configuring the DDNS client, the next step is to configure the DDNS provider. This involves registering with a DDNS provider, providing the necessary credentials, and setting the update intervals for IP address changes.

Step 1: Registering with the DDNS Provider

Sign up with a DDNS service provider (e.g., No-IP, DynDNS, DuckDNS).

After registration, you'll be given access to a user interface where you can create and manage subdomains.

Choose a subdomain (e.g., yourdomain.no-ip.org) that you want to update dynamically.

Step 2: Updating the Server with Login Credentials and Dynamic IP Update Intervals

Once registered, obtain the credentials for your DDNS account, such as the username, password, and subdomain.

In the ddclient.conf file (on your server), provide these details as shown in the configuration section.

Step 3: Setting Update Intervals

You can control how frequently the DDNS service checks for IP address changes by configuring intervals in the ddclient configuration. Typically, DDNS services recommend checking the IP every 5 to 10 minutes. The cron job setup already defines this interval.

Automating DDNS Updates with Cron

To ensure that your DDNS records stay updated, use cron to periodically check for IP address changes and update the DDNS provider. Setting up a cron job to run ddclient every 5 minutes is a common practice.

Steps to Automate DDNS Updates:

Set up a cron job (crontab -e) to run the ddclient command.

Add an entry like:

```
*/5 * * * * /usr/sbin/ddclient -daemon 300 -syslog
```

This ensures that ddclient runs every 5 minutes and updates the DNS records if the IP has changed.

Verifying DDNS Update with dig or nslookup

After configuring everything, you should verify that your DDNS client is working properly. Use either dig or nslookup to check if the domain name resolves to the correct dynamic IP address.

Use dig:

```
dig yourdomain.no-ip.org
```

Use nslookup:

nslookup yourdomain.no-ip.org

These tools will show the IP address associated with your DDNS domain. If everything is configured correctly, you should see the current public IP address of your home network.

By setting up a DDNS client on your server, you can ensure that your domain name always points to your current dynamic IP address, enabling reliable remote access to your network. This process involves installing ddclient (or a similar tool), configuring it with your DDNS provider, and automating the updates using cron. Finally, you can verify the setup by checking the DNS resolution with dig or nslookup to ensure everything is working as expected.

Chapter 6: Advanced Networking Features

Setting Up VPN on a Linux Server Acting as a Router

Setting up a VPN on a Linux server that is acting as a router can provide secure remote access to your network. This setup allows you to route traffic securely from external clients (like laptops or mobile devices) to your internal network via an encrypted tunnel, ensuring confidentiality and integrity of your data. It also enables the routing of network traffic between different networks over a VPN.

Here's a step-by-step guide to set up a VPN on a Linux server acting as a router.

Prerequisites

Before proceeding, ensure the following:

You have a Linux server running and configured as a router (i.e., it is forwarding traffic between interfaces).

You have root or sudo privileges on the server.

A public IP address for your server (or a dynamic DNS setup if your IP is dynamic).

Network address translation (NAT) and IP forwarding are enabled.

Step 1: Install VPN Software

The most commonly used VPN protocols on Linux servers are OpenVPN and WireGuard. For this guide, we will use OpenVPN, but the process can be adapted for other VPN solutions.

Installing OpenVPN on Debian/Ubuntu

First, update your package list and install OpenVPN:

sudo apt update

sudo apt install openvpn easy-rsa

Install the iptables and netfilter-persistent packages to manage firewall rules and save them:

sudo apt install iptables-persistent

Installing OpenVPN on CentOS

Install the EPEL repository and then install OpenVPN:

sudo yum install epel-release

sudo yum install openvpn easy-rsa

Install the iptables-services package to manage firewall rules:

sudo yum install iptables-services

Step 2: Enable IP Forwarding

Since the server is acting as a router, IP forwarding needs to be enabled so the server can route traffic between networks.

To enable IP forwarding temporarily, run:

sudo sysctl -w net.ipv4.ip_forward=1

To enable IP forwarding permanently, edit the sysctl.conf file:

sudo nano /etc/sysctl.conf

Find and uncomment (or add) the following line:

net.ipv4.ip_forward=1

Apply the changes by running:

sudo sysctl -p

Step 3: Configure OpenVPN Server

OpenVPN uses a configuration file (server.conf) to set up the VPN server. The following steps guide you through setting up the server.

Generate Server and Client Keys

Before configuring the server, you'll need to generate a Public Key Infrastructure (PKI) for OpenVPN, including a certificate authority (CA), server certificate, and client certificates. This process can be simplified using Easy-RSA.

Set up Easy-RSA for key generation:

make-cadir ~/openvpn-ca

cd ~/openvpn-ca

source vars

./clean-all

./build-ca

./build-key-server server

./build-dh

./build-key client

After the keys are generated, move the files to the appropriate OpenVPN directories:

sudo cp keys/ca.crt keys/server.crt keys/server.key keys/dh2048.pem /etc/openvpn/

Create the client key:

sudo cp keys/client.crt keys/client.key /etc/openvpn/

OpenVPN Server Configuration

Now, create and edit the OpenVPN server configuration file:

sudo nano /etc/openvpn/server.conf

Paste the following configuration into the server.conf file:

port 1194

proto udp

dev tun

ca /etc/openvpn/ca.crt

cert /etc/openvpn/server.crt

key /etc/openvpn/server.key

dh /etc/openvpn/dh2048.pem

server 10.8.0.0 255.255.255.0

ifconfig-pool-persist /var/log/openvpn/ipp.txt

push "redirect-gateway def1 bypass-dhcp"

push "dhcp-option DNS 8.8.8.8"

push "dhcp-option DNS 8.8.4.4"

keepalive 10 120

```
cipher AES-256-CBC

user nobody

group nobody

persist-key

persist-tun

status /var/log/openvpn/status.log

verb 3
```

The server 10.8.0.0 255.255.255.0 directive sets the VPN subnet.

The push "redirect-gateway def1 bypass-dhcp" option ensures all traffic from the client is routed through the VPN.

The push "dhcp-option DNS 8.8.8.8" and push "dhcp-option DNS 8.8.4.4" lines configure the DNS servers for VPN clients.

Enable IP forwarding for VPN traffic and add NAT rules for the VPN subnet in the server's firewall:

```
sudo iptables -t nat -A POSTROUTING -s 10.8.0.0/24 -o eth0 -j MASQUERADE

sudo iptables-save > /etc/iptables/rules.v4
```

Start the OpenVPN server:

sudo systemctl start openvpn@server

sudo systemctl enable openvpn@server

Step 4: Configure Client VPN

To configure a client to connect to the VPN server:

On the client machine, install OpenVPN:

sudo apt install openvpn

Transfer the following files from the server to the client:

ca.crt (CA certificate)

client.crt (Client certificate)

client.key (Client private key)

Create a configuration file (client.ovpn) on the client machine:

client

dev tun

proto udp

remote [Server-IP] 1194

resolv-retry infinite

nobind

user nobody

group nobody

persist-key

persist-tun

ca ca.crt

cert client.crt

key client.key

remote-cert-tls server

cipher AES-256-CBC

verb 3

Connect to the VPN server:

sudo openvpn --config client.ovpn

Step 5: Testing and Troubleshooting

After starting the VPN server, test the connection from the client to ensure everything works as expected.

Use ping and other network tools to verify the VPN connection is established and traffic is routed correctly.

If there are issues, check the OpenVPN logs on the server (/var/log/openvpn/status.log) and client logs for errors.

Step 6: Ensure VPN Starts on Boot

To make OpenVPN start on boot, enable the OpenVPN service:

sudo systemctl enable openvpn@server

For client machines, create a systemd service to start OpenVPN on boot, or configure the VPN client to start at boot via system tools.

By following these steps, you will have successfully set up a VPN server on a Linux router, allowing remote access to your internal network over a secure encrypted tunnel. This setup is particularly useful for home networks or small office environments where you need to access your network resources securely while outside the local network. You can also route other network traffic securely between different subnets or networks over the VPN connection.

Routing VPN Traffic Through the Home Network

Routing VPN traffic through your home network can provide enhanced security, flexibility, and accessibility. This setup allows you to connect to your home network remotely via a VPN (Virtual Private Network) while ensuring that all traffic from remote clients is routed through your home network, providing you with the ability to access local resources and services securely. You can also use your home network as a gateway to the internet, which adds another layer of privacy and security for your external internet activities.

In this guide, we'll discuss how to set up and configure a Linux-based VPN server, acting as a router, to route VPN traffic through the home network.

Prerequisites

To route VPN traffic through your home network, ensure the following:

Linux-based VPN Server: A Linux machine (such as Debian, Ubuntu, or CentOS) configured as a router with OpenVPN or WireGuard installed.

Home Network Gateway: A router or firewall device that provides Internet access to the home network. The Linux VPN server will act as a gateway between the VPN clients and the internet.

VPN Protocol: We'll use OpenVPN in this guide, but the concepts apply to other VPN protocols like WireGuard.

Network Setup: The home network should have static or DHCP-assigned IPs with routing enabled between the home network and the VPN subnet.

Step 1: Enable IP Forwarding on the VPN Server

Since the VPN server will act as a router, it needs to be able to forward traffic between its VPN clients and the rest of the network. This requires enabling IP forwarding.

Enable IP forwarding temporarily:

sudo sysctl -w net.ipv4.ip_forward=1

Enable IP forwarding permanently by editing the sysctl configuration file:

sudo nano /etc/sysctl.conf

Uncomment (or add) the line:

net.ipv4.ip_forward=1

Apply the change:

sudo sysctl -p

Step 2: Configure iptables for NAT (Network Address Translation)

To route traffic from VPN clients to the internet, you'll need to configure Network Address Translation (NAT) on the VPN server. This allows the server to masquerade as the source of outgoing packets, making them appear to originate from the server rather than the client machines.

Set up NAT with iptables: The following command ensures that traffic from the VPN subnet (e.g., 10.8.0.0/24) is NATted to the public IP address of your server (e.g., eth0 is your public-facing interface).

```
sudo iptables -t nat -A POSTROUTING -s 10.8.0.0/24 -o eth0 -j MASQUERADE
```

Save the iptables rules to ensure they persist after a reboot:

On Debian/Ubuntu, install iptables-persistent and save the rules:

```
sudo apt install iptables-persistent
```

```
sudo iptables-save > /etc/iptables/rules.v4
```

On CentOS, save the iptables rules:

```
sudo service iptables save
```

Step 3: OpenVPN Server Configuration

Now that your server is ready to forward traffic, you need to configure OpenVPN to route VPN traffic to the internal network and internet. You can set OpenVPN to push the appropriate routes to the clients to ensure all traffic flows through the VPN server.

Edit the OpenVPN server configuration file (/etc/openvpn/server.conf):

```
sudo nano /etc/openvpn/server.conf
```

Add the following directives to the configuration file:

Push routes to the client: This directs the clients to route all their traffic through the VPN server, including the default route to the internet.

push "redirect-gateway def1"

push "dhcp-option DNS 8.8.8.8"

push "dhcp-option DNS 8.8.4.4"

Configure the VPN subnet: Ensure that the server has an internal subnet for the VPN clients. For example:

server 10.8.0.0 255.255.255.0

Restart the OpenVPN service to apply the changes:

sudo systemctl restart openvpn@server

Step 4: Configure the Home Router

If you want to access your home network resources (e.g., shared files, printers) through the VPN, you'll need to configure routing on your home router to direct traffic from the VPN subnet to the appropriate local network resources.

Set up static routes on your home router, directing traffic for the VPN subnet to your Linux VPN server. For example, if your home network is 192.168.1.0/24 and the VPN subnet is 10.8.0.0/24, add a route to your router that sends traffic destined for 10.8.0.0/24 to your VPN server's local IP address (e.g., 192.168.1.100).

Check if your home router supports this feature. Most consumer-grade routers provide a static routing section where you can configure routes manually.

Step 5: Connect VPN Clients

Clients can now connect to your VPN and route their traffic through your home network.

Client Configuration: Ensure that the client configuration (client.ovpn) includes the server's public IP or dynamic DNS name, along with the necessary VPN credentials and certificates:

client

dev tun

proto udp

remote [Server-IP] 1194

resolv-retry infinite

nobind

user nobody

group nobody

persist-key

persist-tun

ca ca.crt

cert client.crt

key client.key

remote-cert-tls server

cipher AES-256-CBC

verb 3

Start the VPN Client: On the client machine, run:

sudo openvpn --config client.ovpn

Once connected, verify that the client can access both the internet and resources on the home network. You can test this by pinging internal network devices (e.g., ping 192.168.1.1 for the home router) or browsing internal resources.

Step 6: Testing and Troubleshooting

Testing the VPN Connection: Once the VPN client connects, verify that all traffic (including internet traffic) is routed through the VPN. You can use tools like traceroute or curl to test the route. For example, check the client's public IP:

curl ifconfig.me

If the VPN is correctly routing traffic, it should show the public IP address of the VPN server.

Accessing Home Resources: Test accessing local network resources like shared folders, printers, or servers. Ensure your home router is correctly routing the traffic to your VPN subnet.

Check Logs: If there are any issues, check OpenVPN's server and client logs to identify any errors.

Step 7: Ensuring Persistent Configuration

To ensure the VPN configuration persists across reboots, make sure the following:

Enable IP forwarding permanently by modifying /etc/sysctl.conf (as explained in Step 2).

Ensure iptables rules are loaded on boot:

On Debian/Ubuntu, use iptables-persistent to save and restore firewall rules on reboot.

On CentOS, enable iptables to restore rules on boot:

sudo systemctl enable iptables

By following these steps, you will have successfully routed VPN traffic through your home network, allowing remote access to both the internet and your local resources. This setup is ideal for providing secure remote access to home devices or network services, while ensuring all traffic passes through a centralized, secure point. With the right configurations in place, you'll be able to maintain control over the routing of traffic in and out of your network, providing enhanced security for both local and remote users.

Quality of Service (QoS)

Quality of Service (QoS) refers to the ability to manage and prioritize network traffic to ensure the performance of critical applications and services. QoS is particularly important in networks where multiple types of traffic (such as gaming, video streaming, VoIP, or web browsing) share the same connection, as it allows you to prioritize traffic based on its importance, ensuring that time-sensitive services, such as VoIP or online gaming, perform smoothly even when the network is congested.

Setting up QoS helps optimize network bandwidth, reduce latency, and avoid packet loss for high-priority services. In this guide, we'll discuss how to set up traffic prioritization on a Linux server, using the tc (Traffic Control) command.

Understanding QoS

QoS can be broken down into several components:

Traffic Shaping: Limiting the bandwidth available to specific traffic to avoid congestion and ensure fair distribution.

Traffic Policing: Monitoring traffic to ensure it adheres to predefined limits and applying penalties (such as dropping packets or marking traffic).

Traffic Prioritization: Assigning different levels of importance to different types of traffic to ensure that critical traffic (like VoIP or gaming) gets priority over less time-sensitive traffic (like file downloads).

Setting Up Traffic Prioritization for Different Services

Let's say you want to prioritize certain types of traffic on your home server to ensure that gaming and VoIP services work smoothly, even when the network is under heavy load. You can use the tc tool to implement these rules.

Step 1: Install tc (Traffic Control)

tc is part of the iproute2 package, which is usually pre-installed on most Linux distributions. If it's not installed, you can install it using your package manager.

For Debian/Ubuntu:

sudo apt update

sudo apt install iproute2

For CentOS/RHEL:

sudo yum install iproute

Step 2: Set Up Basic Traffic Control with tc

The tc command allows you to create and manage traffic control rules on a network interface. The basic syntax for using tc is as follows:

tc qdisc add dev [interface] root [queueing discipline] [options]

Where:

[interface] is the network interface (e.g., eth0 or wlan0).

[queueing discipline] specifies the method of handling the traffic (e.g., htb for Hierarchical Token Bucket).

[options] specify additional settings, such as the rate limits or priority rules.

Step 3: Creating a Simple QoS Hierarchy

Create a root queueing discipline (qdisc): Start by applying a basic queueing discipline on the interface. For prioritization, you'll typically use the htb (Hierarchical Token Bucket) qdisc.

sudo tc qdisc add dev eth0 root handle 1: htb default 30

Here:

dev eth0 specifies the network interface (replace eth0 with your interface name).

handle 1: assigns a unique handle for this qdisc.

htb is the queueing discipline.

default 30 specifies the default class for traffic that doesn't match other rules.

Create classes within the root qdisc: Classes define traffic categories, and you can assign bandwidth limits to each class. For example, you can define a class for gaming (priority) and another for file downloads (lower priority).

sudo tc class add dev eth0 parent 1: classid 1:10 htb rate 2mbit ceil 2mbit

sudo tc class add dev eth0 parent 1: classid 1:20 htb rate 1mbit ceil 1mbit

sudo tc class add dev eth0 parent 1: classid 1:30 htb rate 512kbit ceil 1mbit

Here:

parent 1: links the classes to the root qdisc.

classid 1:10, classid 1:20, and classid 1:30 assign unique IDs to each class.

rate sets the minimum bandwidth guarantee for each class.

ceil specifies the maximum bandwidth a class can use (when there is spare bandwidth).

Create filters to assign traffic to these classes: Filters are used to classify incoming packets and direct them to the appropriate class. For example, we can classify VoIP traffic (SIP) to the high-priority class (1:10), gaming traffic to a medium-priority class (1:20), and all other traffic to a low-priority class (1:30).

sudo tc filter add dev eth0 parent 1: protocol ip prio 1 u32 match ip dport 5060 0xffff flowid 1:10

```
sudo tc filter add dev eth0 parent 1: protocol ip prio 2 u32
match ip sport 3478 0xffff flowid 1:20
```

```
sudo tc filter add dev eth0 parent 1: protocol ip prio 3 u32
match ip dport 80 0xffff flowid 1:30
```

Here:

The match ip dport 5060 0xffff filter matches all traffic on port 5060 (typically used for SIP/VoIP).

The match ip sport 3478 0xffff filter matches traffic on port 3478 (used for gaming, e.g., Xbox Live).

The match ip dport 80 0xffff filter matches HTTP traffic.

The prio value sets the priority of the filter, with 1 being the highest.

Step 4: Configuring QoS for Specific Services

You can configure QoS for different services based on their specific port numbers or IP addresses. Here's an example for prioritizing VoIP and gaming traffic:

VoIP: Ensure that VoIP traffic has the highest priority, as it is sensitive to delay and packet loss. Use SIP ports (5060) and RTP ports (typically 10000–20000).

Gaming: Assign a medium priority to gaming traffic (such as Xbox Live or PlayStation Network), which often uses specific ports like 3478–3479 for UDP traffic.

HTTP/HTTPS: Standard web traffic can have a lower priority, as it's less sensitive to slight delays.

Step 5: Monitoring Traffic with tc

To view the current traffic control setup and ensure that your rules are applied correctly, you can use the following commands:

View the qdisc status:

sudo tc qdisc show dev eth0

View class statistics:

sudo tc class show dev eth0

View filter rules:

sudo tc filter show dev eth0

These commands will help you monitor the traffic and see how much data is being processed in each class, as well as the rules being applied.

Step 6: Saving and Restoring QoS Configuration

To make your QoS configuration persistent across reboots, you need to save your tc settings. You can create a script that re-applies the tc configuration after reboot:

Create a script (e.g., /etc/network/if-up.d/qos.sh) and add your tc commands inside it.

```bash
#!/bin/bash

tc qdisc add dev eth0 root handle 1: htb default 30

tc class add dev eth0 parent 1: classid 1:10 htb rate 2mbit
ceil 2mbit

tc class add dev eth0 parent 1: classid 1:20 htb rate 1mbit
ceil 1mbit

tc class add dev eth0 parent 1: classid 1:30 htb rate 512kbit
ceil 1mbit

tc filter add dev eth0 parent 1: protocol ip prio 1 u32 match
ip dport 5060 0xffff flowid 1:10

tc filter add dev eth0 parent 1: protocol ip prio 2 u32 match
ip sport 3478 0xffff flowid 1:20

tc filter add dev eth0 parent 1: protocol ip prio 3 u32 match
ip dport 80 0xffff flowid 1:30
```

Make the script executable:

```bash
sudo chmod +x /etc/network/if-up.d/qos.sh
```

Now, every time the network interface is brought up, the
QoS configuration will be applied automatically.

Quality of Service (QoS) allows you to prioritize critical
services like VoIP and gaming while ensuring that other
traffic, like file downloads or web browsing, doesn't hog the
network bandwidth. By using tc (Traffic Control), you can
configure sophisticated traffic shaping and prioritization
rules to guarantee that high-priority services perform

optimally, even in congested networks. This is an essential feature for ensuring a smooth and responsive network experience for services that require low latency and consistent bandwidth.

Chapter 7: Monitoring and Maintaining Your Server

Monitoring Network Traffic

Monitoring network traffic is an essential task for network administrators and home users alike to ensure the efficient operation of a network. It allows you to track bandwidth usage, identify unusual traffic patterns, troubleshoot network issues, and detect potential security threats like malware or unauthorized access. In this section, we'll look at three popular tools for monitoring network traffic on a Linux system—iftop, nload, and vnstat—as well as how to detect unusual or malicious traffic.

Using iftop to Monitor Real-Time Traffic

iftop is a command-line tool that provides a real-time view of network traffic on an interface. It shows information about which hosts are using the most bandwidth and what connections are active, giving you an overview of your network's activity.

Installing iftop

On **Debian/Ubuntu**:

sudo apt update

sudo apt install iftop

On **CentOS/RHEL**:

sudo yum install iftop

Using iftop

Once installed, simply run iftop with the following command:

sudo iftop

This will display a list of active connections, sorted by the amount of data they are transmitting. Key columns in the iftop output include:

Source/Destination IP and Ports: Shows the remote IP addresses and ports involved in the traffic.

TX/RX (Transmit/Receive): Displays the data rate for the traffic in both directions.

Total Data: Shows the total amount of data transferred during the session.

You can filter traffic by specific ports or IPs using interactive commands. For instance, you can press f to filter by IP address and p to filter by port.

Identifying Unusual Traffic

With iftop, you can easily spot unusual or suspicious traffic. For example, if you notice an unusually high amount of bandwidth being used by a single connection or an unexpected IP address, this could indicate a potential issue or malicious activity, such as a DDoS attack, botnet traffic, or a compromised service on your network.

Using nload for Real-Time Bandwidth Monitoring

nload is another real-time monitoring tool, but it focuses on providing a visual representation of network traffic in terms of bandwidth usage, both incoming and outgoing. Unlike iftop, nload gives you a graphical view of traffic, making it easier to spot spikes or unusual usage trends over time.

Installing nload

On **Debian/Ubuntu**:

sudo apt update

sudo apt install nload

On **CentOS/RHEL**:

sudo yum install nload

Using nload

To start monitoring traffic with nload, simply run:

sudo nload

You will see graphs showing incoming and outgoing traffic in real-time. The graphs can help you visually detect periods of high traffic. If one of your graphs spikes unexpectedly, it could indicate a sudden surge in traffic, which might be caused by a legitimate service or could be a symptom of an attack, such as a DDoS or data exfiltration.

Detecting Malicious Traffic

Unusual spikes in outgoing traffic: Large amounts of outgoing traffic might suggest a compromised machine sending out data without your knowledge, such as in the case of data exfiltration or botnets.

Unexplained traffic at odd times: Traffic spikes during off-hours can be an indicator of malicious activity, such as an internal network compromise or automated botnet attacks.

Using vnstat for Long-Term Traffic Statistics

vnstat is a network traffic monitor that keeps track of traffic statistics for network interfaces over time. Unlike iftop and nload, which focus on real-time monitoring, vnstat allows you to track traffic usage over days, weeks, or months. This long-term data is useful for analyzing bandwidth usage trends and detecting any anomalies or sudden changes.

Installing vnstat

On **Debian/Ubuntu**:

sudo apt update

sudo apt install vnstat

On **CentOS/RHEL**:

sudo yum install vnstat

Using vnstat

Once installed, you can start monitoring your network interface by initializing the database for the network interface. For example, for interface eth0:

sudo vnstat -u -i eth0

To view traffic statistics, run:

vnstat -i eth0

This will show the amount of data transmitted over a specific period, including hourly, daily, weekly, and monthly totals.

Analyzing Traffic Trends

With vnstat, you can identify long-term trends in network traffic. For example, if you notice an unexplained increase in monthly data usage, it could be an indicator of an issue, such as a malware infection or unauthorized large file transfers.

You can also use vnstat in combination with cron to generate daily or weekly reports, which can be useful for identifying spikes or unusual patterns over time.

Detecting Unusual or Malicious Traffic

To detect malicious or unusual traffic using these tools, look for the following signs:

Excessive Outgoing Traffic: A sudden increase in outgoing traffic may be an indicator of a compromised system or data being exfiltrated.

Traffic on Unusual Ports: Unexplained traffic on unusual ports, especially if the traffic volume is high, could indicate malicious activity such as a botnet or malware.

Unusual IP Addresses: Connections to foreign or unknown IP addresses can be a sign of a system breach, as attackers may be trying to send stolen data or exploit vulnerabilities.

Traffic Spikes at Odd Hours: If traffic spikes at odd times, it could be a sign of an automated attack, such as a brute-force attempt or denial-of-service (DoS) attack.

Additional Tools for Security Monitoring

While iftop, nload, and vnstat are useful for monitoring network traffic, there are additional tools that can help detect and analyze malicious traffic:

Wireshark: A packet analyzer that lets you capture and analyze network packets in detail. It's useful for understanding the specifics of network protocols and detecting unusual patterns in traffic.

netstat: Displays network connections, routing tables, interface statistics, and more, which can help you identify active connections or unauthorized services running on your system.

Snort: An open-source intrusion detection system (IDS) that can be used to monitor network traffic for malicious activity.

Suricata: Another IDS that can analyze network traffic in real-time, looking for signs of intrusion or suspicious activity.

Monitoring network traffic is crucial for ensuring the integrity, security, and performance of a network. Using tools like iftop, nload, and vnstat, you can monitor real-time and long-term traffic patterns, enabling you to detect unusual or malicious behavior. By regularly reviewing your network activity and identifying signs of suspicious traffic— such as unexpected outgoing traffic, unknown IP addresses, or unusual spikes—you can quickly respond to potential security threats and protect your system.

Regular Maintenance

Regular Maintenance for Network Security and Server Health

Regular maintenance is critical to ensure that your Linux server, including network services and firewall configurations, remains secure, efficient, and reliable. This involves routine updates, monitoring, backups, and ensuring that your server is running optimally. Key maintenance tasks for firewall security and server management include updating firewall rules, regularly updating Linux packages, and backing up configuration files and logs. In this section, we'll explore these key maintenance activities in detail.

Updating Firewall Rules Regularly

As your network configuration changes, so too should your firewall rules. Regularly updating your firewall rules ensures that new services, ports, and protocols are properly protected, and old, unused rules are removed to maintain efficiency. It also helps to adapt to evolving security threats by ensuring your rules block the latest known vulnerabilities.

Why Update Firewall Rules?

Adapting to Network Changes: As new services are added, or configurations change, your firewall needs to reflect these changes to ensure proper security controls.

Blocking Emerging Threats: New exploits and vulnerabilities are discovered regularly. Updating firewall rules helps mitigate the risk of these vulnerabilities being exploited by attackers.

Optimizing Network Traffic: Removing unnecessary rules or consolidating redundant ones can improve firewall performance and ensure traffic is properly filtered.

How to Update Firewall Rules

Reviewing Existing Rules: Periodically review your current firewall rules. Use commands like iptables -L or firewalld to list all active rules and look for any outdated or redundant configurations.

Testing New Rules: Before applying new firewall rules, test them in a controlled environment to avoid inadvertently blocking critical services.

Implementing Changes: After reviewing and testing the rules, apply the changes. On systems using iptables, you can save the new rule set using:

sudo iptables-save > /etc/iptables/rules.v4

For systems using firewalld, update the firewall-cmd configuration with new or modified rules:

sudo firewall-cmd --permanent --add-port=XXXX/tcp

sudo firewall-cmd --reload

Automation: Consider automating rule updates where possible, using scripts or configuration management tools (such as Ansible or Puppet) to keep your firewall rules in sync with your server's network configuration.

Updating Linux Packages Regularly

Keeping your Linux packages updated is essential for maintaining the security and stability of your system. Linux distributions often release security patches and updates to address vulnerabilities, improve performance, and add new features. Failing to regularly update packages can leave your system open to exploits.

Why Update Linux Packages?

Security Patches: New vulnerabilities are discovered frequently. Updating packages ensures your system is protected against exploits.

Bug Fixes: Updates often fix bugs that could cause instability, crashes, or security weaknesses.

Performance Improvements: Software updates may include optimizations that improve server performance, reduce resource usage, or enhance network reliability.

New Features: Keeping packages up to date ensures you have access to the latest features and improvements in the tools you are using.

How to Update Packages

Debian/Ubuntu:

Update package lists:

sudo apt update

Upgrade installed packages:

sudo apt upgrade

Optionally, perform a full upgrade (including removing obsolete packages):

sudo apt full-upgrade

Clean up unused packages:

sudo apt autoremove

CentOS/RHEL:

Update package lists and upgrade installed packages:

sudo yum update

Clean up unused packages:

sudo yum autoremove

Automation: You can automate the update process by using cron jobs or systemd timers to periodically check for and install updates. For example, to automatically update packages on a Debian/Ubuntu server:

Install unattended-upgrades:

sudo apt install unattended-upgrades

Enable automatic updates:

sudo dpkg-reconfigure --priority=low unattended-upgrades

Backing Up Configuration Files and Logs

Backing up important configuration files and logs is a key aspect of system maintenance. These backups serve as a safety net in case of accidental changes, system failures, or security breaches. If your firewall configuration, network settings, or system packages are modified or corrupted, backups allow you to restore the system to its previous state quickly.

Why Backup Configuration Files and Logs?

Restore Critical Settings: Configuration files control the behavior of your server and services. Losing or corrupting these files can make it difficult to restore functionality.

Disaster Recovery: In the event of system failure, you can restore configurations and logs without needing to manually reconfigure each service.

Auditing and Troubleshooting: Log files provide valuable information for auditing and troubleshooting. Regularly backing up these logs ensures you retain a history of activities on your server.

Key Files to Backup

Firewall Rules: Save your firewall configuration files (e.g., /etc/iptables/rules.v4 for iptables or /etc/firewalld/zones/ for firewalld).

System Configuration Files: Backup /etc/network/interfaces (for network configuration) and /etc/sysctl.conf (for system parameters).

Service Configurations: Save configurations for web servers (e.g., /etc/apache2/, /etc/nginx/) or databases (e.g., /etc/mysql/).

Log Files: Ensure that system and application logs, often located in /var/log/, are backed up regularly. Important logs include syslog, auth.log, and web server logs.

How to Backup Configuration Files and Logs

Manual Backup: Use simple commands like cp or rsync to copy important files to a backup directory:

sudo cp /etc/iptables/rules.v4 /path/to/backup/iptables-rules-backup

sudo cp /var/log/syslog /path/to/backup/syslog-backup

Automated Backups: Set up cron jobs to back up configuration files and logs regularly. For example:

Create a backup script (/usr/local/bin/backup-config.sh):

#!/bin/bash

cp /etc/iptables/rules.v4 /path/to/backup/iptables-rules-backup

cp /var/log/syslog /path/to/backup/syslog-backup

Set up a cron job to run the script daily:

sudo crontab -e

Add the following line to schedule the backup at 2 am every day

0 2 * * * /usr/local/bin/backup-config.sh

Backup with Rsync: You can also use rsync to synchronize configuration files and logs to a remote server or backup location:

sudo rsync -av /etc/iptables/rules.v4

user@backupserver:/path/to/backup/

sudo rsync -av /var/log/ user@backupserver:/path/to/logs-backup/

Regular maintenance is essential to ensure your Linux server remains secure, functional, and efficient. By regularly updating firewall rules and system packages, and backing up crucial configuration files and logs, you can reduce the risk of security breaches, ensure high availability, and be prepared to quickly recover from failures. Taking the time to implement a solid maintenance routine will help you maintain a stable and secure network environment.

Appendix

Common iptables Commands

Viewing Existing Rules

List all rules:

sudo iptables -L

List rules in a specific chain (e.g., INPUT):

sudo iptables -L INPUT

Display rules with line numbers (helpful for rule deletion):

sudo iptables -L --line-numbers

List rules with more detailed output (including packet and byte counts):

sudo iptables -L -v

Display rules with the specific table (e.g., NAT table):

sudo iptables -t nat -L

Adding, Deleting, and Modifying Rules

Append a rule (add a rule to the end of a chain):

sudo iptables -A INPUT -p tcp --dport 80 -j ACCEPT

This allows incoming traffic on port 80 (HTTP).

Insert a rule (add a rule to the beginning of a chain):

sudo iptables -I INPUT 1 -p tcp --dport 22 -j ACCEPT

This allows incoming traffic on port 22 (SSH) and inserts it at the top of the INPUT chain.

Delete a rule (by specifying line number):

sudo iptables -D INPUT 1

This deletes the rule at line 1 in the INPUT chain.

Delete a specific rule (by specifying the entire rule):

sudo iptables -D INPUT -p tcp --dport 22 -j ACCEPT

Replace a rule (replace a rule at a specific line number):

sudo iptables -R INPUT 1 -p tcp --dport 22 -j DROP

Flushing and Clearing Rules

Flush all rules (delete all rules in the current table):

sudo iptables -F

Flush specific chain (e.g., INPUT):

sudo iptables -F INPUT

Delete all custom chains (if any exist):

sudo iptables -X

Saving and Restoring Rules

Save iptables rules to make them persistent across reboots (Debian/Ubuntu):

sudo iptables-save > /etc/iptables/rules.v4

Restore iptables rules from saved configuration:

sudo iptables-restore < /etc/iptables/rules.v4

Make rules persistent on CentOS/Red Hat (using service):

sudo service iptables save

Managing Traffic with Actions

Accept traffic:

sudo iptables -A INPUT -p tcp --dport 80 -j ACCEPT

This allows incoming HTTP traffic.

Drop traffic (discard the packet without sending a reply):

sudo iptables -A INPUT -p tcp --dport 23 -j DROP

This drops incoming Telnet traffic (port 23).

Reject traffic (responds with an error message to the sender):

sudo iptables -A INPUT -p tcp --dport 23 -j REJECT

This rejects Telnet traffic on port 23.

Port Forwarding (NAT)

Port forwarding example: Forward incoming traffic on port 8080 to an internal IP address (e.g., 192.168.1.100 on port 80):

sudo iptables -t nat -A PREROUTING -p tcp --dport 8080 -j DNAT --to-destination 192.168.1.100:80

```
sudo iptables -A FORWARD -p tcp -d 192.168.1.100 --dport
80 -j ACCEPT
```

Enable IP forwarding (necessary for NAT and routing):

```
sudo sysctl -w net.ipv4.ip_forward=1
```

Blocking Specific IP Addresses

Block a specific IP address:

```
sudo iptables -A INPUT -s 192.168.1.100 -j DROP
```

Block an entire subnet:

```
sudo iptables -A INPUT -s 192.168.1.0/24 -j DROP
```

Limiting and Rate Limiting

Limit SSH connections (to prevent brute-force attacks):

```
sudo iptables -A INPUT -p tcp --dport 22 -m connlimit --
connlimit-above 4 -j REJECT
```

Rate limit connections to prevent DoS attacks:

```
sudo iptables -A INPUT -p tcp --dport 80 -m limit --limit
10/minute --limit-burst 20 -j ACCEPT
```

Logging Traffic

Log dropped packets (helps in debugging and monitoring):

sudo iptables -A INPUT -j LOG --log-prefix "Dropped Packet: " --log-level 4

Limit logging rate (to prevent log floods):

sudo iptables -A INPUT -j LOG --log-prefix "Dropped Packet: " --log-level 4 --limit 5/minute

Specific Protocols and Port Filtering

Allow HTTP traffic (port 80):

sudo iptables -A INPUT -p tcp --dport 80 -j ACCEPT

Allow DNS traffic (port 53):

sudo iptables -A INPUT -p udp --dport 53 -j ACCEPT

Allow ICMP (ping) traffic:

sudo iptables -A INPUT -p icmp --icmp-type echo-request -j ACCEPT

Default Policies

Set the default policy to drop all incoming traffic:

sudo iptables -P INPUT DROP

Set the default policy to accept all incoming traffic:

sudo iptables -P INPUT ACCEPT

Set the default policy to drop all forwarded traffic:

sudo iptables -P FORWARD DROP

Blocking Certain Services

Block a specific port (e.g., port 23 for Telnet):

sudo iptables -A INPUT -p tcp --dport 23 -j REJECT

Block all incoming traffic except for certain services (e.g., allow HTTP, SSH):

sudo iptables -A INPUT -p tcp --dport 22 -j ACCEPT

sudo iptables -A INPUT -p tcp --dport 80 -j ACCEPT

sudo iptables -A INPUT -j DROP

Basic Network Troubleshooting Commands (ping, traceroute, etc.)

ping - Check Connectivity

The ping command is one of the most basic and widely used tools to check network connectivity. It sends Internet Control Message Protocol (ICMP) Echo Request packets to a specified host and waits for a response.

Basic Usage:

ping <hostname or IP address>

Example:

ping google.com

This will send packets to google.com and show how long it takes to receive a reply (in milliseconds). If the destination does not respond, the ping command will indicate a timeout or unreachable host.

Send a specific number of pings:

ping -c 4 google.com

This sends 4 packets and then stops.

Change packet size:

ping -s 1000 google.com

This sends packets of 1000 bytes.

Continuous ping until interrupted:

ping google.com

traceroute - Trace the Route to a Host

The traceroute command traces the path packets take from your computer to a destination host, showing each intermediate hop (router) along the way. This is useful for diagnosing where delays or failures are occurring.

Basic Usage:

traceroute <hostname or IP address>

Example:

traceroute google.com

This command will display the route packets take from your machine to google.com, along with the response time from each hop.

Specifying a maximum number of hops:

traceroute -m 20 google.com

This limits the trace to 20 hops.

Use ICMP Echo Request instead of UDP (more reliable on some networks):

traceroute -I google.com

---

netstat - Display Network Connections and Statistics

The netstat (network statistics) command displays network connections, routing tables, interface statistics, and other network-related information. It's helpful for diagnosing connection issues or identifying unexpected network activity.

List active network connections:

netstat -tuln

This shows active TCP/UDP connections and the ports they are listening on (-t for TCP, -u for UDP, -l for listening, -n for numeric addresses).

Display network statistics:

netstat -i

This shows detailed statistics about network interfaces (e.g., packets sent/received, errors).

List all open sockets and their associated programs:

netstat -tulnp

ifconfig - Display or Configure Network Interfaces

The ifconfig command is used to display or configure network interfaces on your system. It's commonly used to check the status of network interfaces or assign new IP addresses.

Display network interfaces and their IP addresses:

ifconfig

This will list all active interfaces, their IP addresses, netmasks, and other configuration details.

Check the status of a specific interface:

ifconfig eth0

This shows information for the eth0 interface.

Assign a static IP address to an interface (e.g., eth0):

sudo ifconfig eth0 192.168.1.100 netmask 255.255.255.0

ip - Show/Modify Routing, Devices, and Tunnel Information

The ip command is a more modern tool for working with network interfaces, routing tables, and IP addresses. It's typically used instead of ifconfig on newer Linux systems.

Display all network interfaces:

ip a

Display the routing table:

ip route

Show the status of network interfaces:

ip link show

Assign an IP address to an interface:

sudo ip addr add 192.168.1.100/24 dev eth0

nslookup - Query DNS for Information

nslookup is a command-line tool for querying DNS servers to obtain domain name or IP address information. It's helpful for diagnosing DNS issues.

Basic usage to resolve a domain name:

nslookup google.com

This returns the IP address associated with google.com.

Query a specific DNS server:

nslookup google.com 8.8.8.8

This queries Google's public DNS server (8.8.8.8) for the IP address of google.com.

dig - DNS Lookup Tool

dig (Domain Information Groper) is another tool for querying DNS servers, similar to nslookup, but it provides more detailed output.

Basic usage to query a domain:

dig google.com

This provides more detailed information than nslookup, including the query time and the DNS server used.

Query a specific DNS server:

dig @8.8.8.8 google.com

Perform a reverse DNS lookup (find domain name associated with an IP):

dig -x 8.8.8.8

curl - Transfer Data from or to a Server

curl is a command-line tool used to transfer data using various network protocols (HTTP, HTTPS, FTP, etc.). It's useful for testing web server connectivity and checking if a particular service is up.

Check if a web server is reachable:

curl google.com

Fetch HTTP headers:

curl -I google.com

This will display the HTTP headers returned by the server.

Check response time and other details:

curl -v google.com

route - View and Manipulate the Routing Table

The route command shows or manipulates the system's routing table, which determines how packets are forwarded to their destination.

Display the routing table:

route -n

Add a static route (e.g., route traffic destined for 10.1.1.0/24 through gateway 192.168.1.1):

sudo route add -net 10.1.1.0/24 gw 192.168.1.1

netcat (nc) - Network Utility for Reading/Writing Network Connections

netcat (often abbreviated as nc) is a versatile tool that can create TCP or UDP connections and listen on specific ports, useful for debugging and testing network connections.

Listen on a port (e.g., port 1234):

nc -l 1234

Connect to a remote service (e.g., test an HTTP server):

nc google.com 80

Transfer a file over TCP:

nc -l 1234 > received_file.txt

On the sending machine:

nc <destination_ip> 1234 < file_to_send.txt

tcpdump - Capture and Analyze Network Traffic

tcpdump is a powerful packet capture tool used to monitor and analyze network traffic. It helps troubleshoot network issues by inspecting packets transmitted over the network.

Capture packets on a specific interface:

sudo tcpdump -i eth0

Capture traffic on a specific port:

sudo tcpdump -i eth0 port 80

Write captured packets to a file for later analysis:

sudo tcpdump -i eth0 -w capture.pcap